PRAISE FOR *VICTORY LAP RETIREMENT*

"[The authors] say the full-stop retirement doesn't work anymore, and I agree. Start planning your Victory Lap."
— *Rob Carrick, Personal Finance Columnist,*
The Globe and Mail

"I've long believed that the idea of retiring at sixty-five is as outdated as the horse and buggy. You could live another thirty years or more. What are you going to do with that time? This book can help you find the answers."
— *Gordon Pape, Bestselling Author and Publisher of* The Internet Wealth Builder *and* The Income Investor

"This wise book rests on some important truths: We all crave lives of meaning, we want to continue to grow and learn throughout our years, and financial well-being is central to our health and happiness. *Victory Lap Retirement* is a how-to guide for making all of those goals come together into a truly modern retirement plan."
— *Christine Benz, Director of Personal Finance and Senior Columnist, Morningstar, Inc.*

"*Victory Lap Retirement* provides a great model for finding the right balance between today and tomorrow, work and play, family and self, financial independence and fun. It's a brilliant roadmap for being deliberate about your priorities and to avoid ending up just being a cog in the wheel of life. The authors masterfully leverage their personal experience and the lessons learned from working with thousands of clients, bucking the tired old model of retirement and instead offering readers a detailed roadmap to deliberately create a far more meaningful, interesting, and fulfilling second half of life."
— *Brent Brodeski, CEO, Savant Capital Management*

"You don't have to stop working in retirement. You can design an 'encore career' that keeps you from depleting your savings too soon and provides an alternative to doing nothing. Boredom is the elephant in the room, say these authors, who build on their own experiences to help you embark on your own Victory Lap."

—*Ellen Roseman, Personal Finance Journalist, Author, Continuing Education Instructor, and Victory Lap enthusiast*

"The authors reframe the idea of retirement as a smart twist on an age-old dilemma. The science of well-being later in life tells us we need to have a purpose—why not make a few bucks while you're at it? This book will open your mind to what your Victory Lap might be if the thought of doing nothing at some point is foreign to you."

—*Larry Berman, Host of BNN Bloomberg's* Berman's Call, *and Chief Investment Officer, ETF Capital Management*

"I've always believed once you have your financial house in order it would free you up to do the things you love to do and would give your life more meaning and balance. Imagine the luxury of working because you want to, not because you have to. No one wants life to become a series of takeaways. Stay in the game. Enjoy and thrive during your 'Victory Lap.'"

—*Patricia Lovett-Reid, Chief Financial Commentator, CTV News*

"Personally, I never want to retire. I was happy to read I'm not alone. In fact, continuing to work may extend my life (and yours). The value of *Victory Lap Retirement* transcends the benefit of working longer. This book makes a valuable contribution to investors. It's easy to read and the recommendations are simple to implement. I highly recommend it."

—*Dan Solin, Author of "The Smartest . . ." series of investing books*

"A 'new age' approach to enjoying a more fulfilling and sustainable retirement lifestyle that you can embrace, customize and implement. Bravo!"

—*Daryl Diamond, Author of* Your Retirement Income Blueprint

"This book truly resonated with me. I personally experienced 'Sudden Retirement Syndrome' until I created my own Victory Lap. . . . This is a must-read for people of any age planning their lifecycles."
    —*Dr. Sherry Cooper, Chief Economist, Dominion Lending Centres; Former Executive Vice-President and Chief Economist, BMO Financial Group*

"Too many of us treat financial independence as the end game, but that's the wrong approach; [it] should be seen as the start line of a new chapter of life. . . . *Victory Lap Retirement* focuses on life after financial independence and how to create and maintain a healthy, satisfying, and self-fulfilling lifestyle. Easy and informative to read, everyone working toward financial independence should read *Victory Lap Retirement.*"
    —*Tawcan from www.tawcan.com, Early-Retirement Blogger*

"Informative and entertaining . . . *Victory Lap* is a fun book that everyone of all ages should read."
    —Diane Francis, *National Post* Editor-at-Large

"Jon and I have had many stimulating discussions about our parallel 'working retirements.' I urge everyone to read *Victory Lap Retirement* to discover how . . . this will free you financially so you can embrace an encore career that will make you jump out of bed every morning with a smile on your face."
    —*Sheryl Smolkin, Journalist, Pension Lawyer*

"[This] primer on how to transition to retirement by outlining how to work while you play is full of helpful tips on how to align habits with long-term goals. You'll be richer for reading it."
    —*Julie Cazzin, Senior Editor,* MoneySense

"Like pioneers documenting their personal journey into the new uncharted lands of redesigning retirement, these authors offer valuable insights and survival strategies to help properly prepare those who will follow in their quest to this new frontier."
    —*Doug Dahmer, Founder, Emeritus Retirement Income Specialists*

VICTORY LAP
RETIREMENT

VICTORY LAP RETIREMENT

Work While You Play, Play While You Work

SECOND EDITION

MIKE DRAK
ROB MORRISON, CFP®
JONATHAN CHEVREAU

MILNER &
ASSOCIATES INC
· EDITING · PUBLISHING · COMMUNICATIONS · CONSULTING ·

ISBN 978-1-988344-12-6 (paperback)
ISBN 978-1-988344-15-7 (e-book)

Production Credits

Editor and project manager: Karen Milner
Copy editor: Lindsay Humphreys
Interior design and typesetting: Adrian So, adriansodesign.com
Cover design: Adrian So, Adrian So Design
Printer: Friesens

Published by Milner & Associates Inc.
www.milnerassociates.ca

Printed in Canada
10 9 8 7 6 5 4 3 2 1

To our fellow baby boomers. It's finally our turn again.
What are you waiting for?

Contents

Foreword

by Ernie Zelinski

Having spent over half of my adult life in the business of personal development, mainly related to leisure and retirement, I have often been asked, "What is the secret to enjoying retirement to the fullest?" In other words, what can we do to make the years ahead of us satisfying and meaningful? To be sure, this is an important question. It is a particularly important question to ask ourselves as we approach the so-called retirement age. In fact, it's a worthwhile question to ask ourselves at any stage in life. Another key question is, "How can we transition from work to retirement in an easy and stress-free manner?" This is where *Victory Lap Retirement* valiantly enters the picture. It answers both questions by reawakening us to what truly matters in our lives and showing us the path toward creating a low-stress, healthy, vibrant lifestyle.

Mike, Jonathan, and Rob will help you rethink what retirement means to you, particularly if you tend to think of it in the

traditional sense. After giving the subject of retirement some serious thought themselves, and also doing some intensive research
on it, these three authors have come up with a new perspective on
how to manifest your grandest desires, transitioning from your
main career into a life of more leisure combined with satisfying
pursuits.

An unknown wise person once proclaimed, "Retirement is
wonderful if you have two essentials—much to live on and much
to live for." The keys to attracting these two important elements
of retirement are in the pages of this book. *Victory Lap Retirement*
is not only for those considering their retirement, but also for
anyone interested in the pursuit of happiness, satisfaction, and
self-actualization.

Many of the books and magazines that discuss retirement focus on building a nest egg, investing, and accumulating wealth.
To be sure, this book offers helpful financial advice; but it com-
prises so much more than financial planning because the authors
know that happiness during retirement is largely dependent upon
other factors: having good health, good friends, and a variety of
interests.

The traditional retirement-planning industry falls short on
providing retirement-planning tools that help us realize what
truly matters most about our lives and our retirement. The new
retirement-planning model requires new styles of planning and
preparedness, and that is what you'll find in *Victory Lap Retirement*.
This masterpiece provides powerful tips, techniques, and secrets
that can transform a boring, traditional retirement into an exciting one, including:

- How to put yourself firmly in command of your own
  financial destiny

- How to acquire wealth and how to manage it as it grows
- How to enjoy retirement regardless of your financial situation
- How to realize a deep new love for life
- How to free yourself from the burden of fearing traditional retirement
- How to create a life you don't have to retire from
- How to use your time wisely
- The importance of true freedom, which is not being imprisoned by money and material possessions
- What makes us happy, and focusing on that instead of on what wastes our time and energy
- How to give life to your dreams

If you have ever longed to have more, to experience more, to *be* more than you ever imagined being in your later years—possibly even more than you have ever been at any other time in your life—then *Victory Lap Retirement* is the book for you. The information and tools provided within its pages will vastly increase your chances of attaining the life you envision. The authors emphasize that retirement is not a time to rest. Retirement, instead, is a time to be active, to learn, and to explore; maybe even a time to start a new, fun career. Whether your finances allow you to travel or have a vacation home, or require you to learn to live on less, you have many opportunities for living a decent and satisfying life.

In short, this book offers you a brilliant blueprint for enhancing your life financially, emotionally, intellectually, physically, and spiritually. It will inspire you still to be traveling, painting, taking photographs, and doing many other satisfying activities well into your seventies, eighties, and beyond, particularly if you still have good health. So allow Jonathan, Mike, and Rob to lead you on a journey of self-discovery and renewal in the pages of this book, which will help make your life better than ever.

Ernie J. Zelinski
"Helping Adventurous Souls Live Prosperous and Free"
International best-selling author of *How to Retire Happy, Wild, and Free* (over 275,000 copies sold and published in nine languages) and *The Joy of Not Working* (over 285,000 copies sold and published in seventeen languages)

Introduction

Victory Lap Retirement was originally published in October 2016 and already we have done a revision. It's a lot of work, but we are willing to do it as we're on a bit of a crusade to change the way our society thinks about and practices retirement. Why? Because the old, traditional retirement model is outdated and no longer works.

We also picked up another co-author along the way, a like-minded colleague who thinks about retirement the same way we do. Rob Morrison is a practicing financial adviser in the Chicago area, working with clients transitioning into and through retirement. He became fascinated with transitional retirement many years ago (also calling it Glidepath retirement) through client experiences, and has been championing the concept ever since, coincidentally under the same name in recent years: Victory Lap. It made all the sense in the world to join forces on this worthy crusade to change our collective world view about retirement!

We have learned from talking to retirees at our retirement seminars, through our blog, and from Rob's clients at his financial advisory firm that many baby boomers feel that 65 is way too young to transition to a life of pure leisure, and maybe way too old to begin getting some more balance in life. They realize that they may live another thirty years and they need to find a way to pay for such an extended retirement; unless you have the benefit of substantial assets to support you, maintaining a source of active income for as long as you can is the prudent way to go in order to mitigate retirement risk. Secondly, the boomers who are retiring today know that thirty years is a little bit long to sit on the porch and watch the world go by. The key is to stay engaged, to find work that you like to do and that gives you the flexibility you require.

For many years, the media and even the financial industry have been telling us the wrong story; a happy retirement is not simply about ceasing to work. In fact, most retirees today don't want to spend the remainder of their days just sitting on a beach relaxing or out on the golf course. They don't want to quit and *not work* because, after a lifetime of working, that feels unnatural to them. How do you replace the sense of achievement from having done a job well, or the positive feelings derived from socializing with co-workers?

People like us want *purpose*, because without purpose we know that we might go a little stir crazy, like some of our retired friends who attempt to escape the boredom they feel with TV, drugs, alcohol, social media, gambling, and buying stuff on credit that they really don't need.

Successful retirees have increased awareness and know that contributing to a business or other organization or cause, via paid employment or volunteer work, makes them feel good and can reduce the risks of stroke, dementia, mobility issues, disability, and premature death.

What people like us want is less stress and more flexibility—we want to stay engaged with meaningful work of some kind, but in a limited way and on our own terms. Working three days a week, for example, or maybe six months a year, so we can also accommodate multiple commitments, such as caring for grandchildren and elderly parents, and allowing us time to pursue other passions and interests.

Check out the numbers for yourself. According to an article called "It's Time to Retire Retirement" in the March 2004 issue of the *Harvard Business Review*, "Twenty percent of those collecting employer pensions are still working in some capacity, and among people under 60 who are already collecting pensions, more than 50% are working. Among those age 55 and older who accepted early retirement offers, one-third have gone back to work. But these working retirees are more likely to be working part-time or be self-employed than their not-yet-retired counterparts—in other words, they're working on their own terms."

The bottom line is that people like us want to continue working past normal retirement age, both for financial and non-financial reasons. In fact, working to some degree and in some capacity may be better for your overall health, longevity, fulfillment, and peace of mind.

FINANCIAL REASONS FOR CONTINUING TO WORK

Retirement should not be merely about holding on and surviving. It should be about staying engaged and having fun, but active retirements can be expensive, especially if you plan on doing a lot of traveling.

If you can't afford to go out and see a show, if you can't afford to go where you want on vacation, and if you can only afford to go see your grandkids at least once a year at Thanksgiving, retirement will be incredibly disappointing, and that is why many boomers want or need at least a part-time job.

Continuing to work will also allow you to help your children and grandchildren financially if you so choose. Life today is hard; there is no denying that the high cost of education and housing is putting a lot of stress on our kids. It's ok for you to serve as a safety net in time of need, just make sure that by helping you're not compromising your own retirement future.

It's a big mistake to retire full stop and think that you will just figure it out as you go. It's stressful continually hoping that you won't run out of money, that the government won't mess with Social Security; worrying about the impact of inflation, and being able to afford the rising cost of health care.

You'll save yourself a lot of anxiety and sleep better at night if you know where you stand financially, and where your monthly income is coming from. After doing your homework you may find that to enjoy the retirement lifestyle you dream of, you will need to save more, cut back on some planned expenses, or work longer; but, if we have done our job right, at least you should be clear-eyed about your priorities after reading this book and will know what you need to do.

NON-FINANCIAL REASONS FOR CONTINUING TO WORK

Watch the movie *The Intern* and you will learn a lot about the non-financial benefits of continuing to work. The plot follows Ben Whittaker (Robert De Niro) a well off, seventy-year-old widower who becomes a senior intern at an online fashion website. He doesn't need the money but looks at his new job as the perfect solution for the loneliness he has been feeling since his wife died.

His work makes him feel that he still matters and it makes him happy to be part of something again. He becomes something of a father figure to several of the younger workers by offering advice about issues such as love, clothes sense, and work-life balance. Also, many of the daily challenges he faces in learning new technology and problem solving keep his mental faculties sharp. The job also keeps him socially active and results in him making many new friends.

You might have a new appreciation for the value of working in retirement after watching this movie.

• • •

Whether financial reasons or non-financial factors, or both, are motivating you to plan for an active retirement that includes work in some form, we call that a Victory Lap. This concept covers any picture of retirement that keeps you engaged and in the game. A Victory Lap most commonly describes the slow, victorious circuit taken by an athlete of any track, playing field, or sheet of ice after winning a race or other sporting contest. It's that extra, happy time of continuing to run, bike or skate, but it's done in a different way and at an entirely different pace. It's an opportunity to bask in the glory and enjoy the fruits of months or years of training, practice, and sacrifice.

A Victory Lap occurs after the main event, as it were. It's a continuation of a race or sporting event that's sort of the same as, but mostly different than, what came before. Similarly, our version of the concept, *Victory Lap Retirement*, refers to a new stage of life between the traditional salaried "primary" career and the end-game of "full-stop" retirement. You may continue to work after your full-time employment, but in a different way and at a different pace; and you'll be able to enjoy much more leisure time than at any time of your life before that.

A Victory Lap is a complete, all-round lifestyle that each person designs for himself or herself. The idea is to create an ideal blend of work and play (hence this book's subtitle). You'll see from the table of contents that we also include chapters on health, time, and spiritual health, for example, in addition to chapters concerned with work and more strictly financial matters.

The benefits of the more holistic philosophy of Victory Lap Retirement are many. It can actually help to improve the overall quality of the rest of your life and, by extension, the lives of your loved ones. Who doesn't want to live a longer, healthier, and more productive life? Who doesn't want to manifest their innermost dreams and achieve goals long suppressed while spending decades raising a family and building wealth?

•   •   •

Older baby boomers may already be leaving corporate life in their late fifties or early sixties, but few are ready to hang up their skates and settle for a passive life of watching daytime television, or playing golf. They didn't come this far to retire in the traditional sense. They know they need more if they are going to be happy.

The essence of Victory Lap Retirement is to leave corporate employment, which usually entails working for someone else, and enter a new and different phase of your life. This may mean working for yourself, but it could also simply mean continuing to keep the little gray cells active in some other endeavor—hopefully in a way that supplements whatever pension and retirement income you've generated as a result of decades of "slaving and saving."

There are all kinds of Victory Lap Retirements. Some may pursue a traditional retirement but keep their hand in the workforce by working just a few days a week. Others will make the leap from the corporate cubicle to self-employment strictly to generate what we call a "playcheck." That's a bit of extra fun money that can be spent guilt-free on little luxuries or experiences as opposed to accumulating more "stuff." For example, Jonathan's friend Meta is north of 100 but still works two half-days a week so she can take one-day excursions to attend plays or visit wineries.

However you choose to design your Victory Lap Retirement, it should provide a huge amount of flexibility compared to the nine-to-five corporate grind. You're now your own boss and can work as much or as little as you wish, as you craft a lifestyle that best combines the elements of work and play that appeal to your unique personality. Your days are now dictated by your personal passions and goals that you may have put off during your time in the cubicle. You may still be earning money, but what you're doing will be slightly or completely different than your old career. Odds are you will find this new phase of your life much more fulfilling.

For baby boomers and those that follow them, we believe the best is yet to come. In our own circles we can think of a financial adviser who has become an actor, a rock star who became an Anglican minister, and a pension expert who now runs a retirement website.

The boomers may be corporate refugees now, but few of us are ready to get off the track and plonk down in the easy chair for the rest of our lives. We may not be running flat out anymore or marching to the tune of some corporate boss half our age, but we're hardly done yet.

Welcome to Victory Lap Retirement!

1

Rethinking Retirement

If I knew I was going to live this long, I'd have taken better care of myself.
—Mickey Mantle

Today the word "retirement" is being widely misused and fails to describe exactly what life looks like for people in their fifties, sixties, seventies, and beyond. To understand the issue fully, it's helpful to look back on a brief history of retirement—how that system came to be, and what that way of life typically has looked like.

Retirement as we know it today did not exist prior to the industrialization of various Western democracies. People lived on farms just like on the television show *The Waltons*. Farmers didn't retire, and the responsibility of older farmers was to pass on their knowledge and skills to the next generation. In return, the sons and daughters accepted the responsibility to provide care to the elderly, which was payback for the parents raising them. Life was a lot simpler back then.

Industrialization and the lure of a better life in cities resulted in people shifting from a life of self-sufficiency to a life of dependency on their employers. This shift came at a cost, as the new factory worker gave up a way of life that was in itself satisfying, trading a life where he was in control for a future where he would be a small cog in a large machine.

Along with industrialization came the eventual creation of Social Security in the United States. Launched in 1935, Social Security was designed to support the older worker who, on average, didn't have that many years left to live. The viability of Social Security counted on the assumption that the majority of retirees would die within a few years of starting retirement.

So everyone had the same goal: you worked hard for thirty-five years, and then, if you were one of the lucky ones to actually reach the finish line, you could finally stop working and enjoy a few years of passive leisure. We use the term "passive leisure" here, as most people back then were not in robust enough health to partake in active leisure. So it's easy to see why people would link "not working" to retirement, as it was the natural progression at the time: stop working = rocking chair. The literal definition of "retire" is to withdraw, to retreat, to shut oneself away. This definition was an appropriate fit for what was happening at that time.

Then a funny thing happened: people started to live longer. And they weren't just living longer, they were also healthier and more active in those later years. For evidence of this, visit any community recreation center and you will be amazed at the number of baby boomers working out, taking aerobic or yoga classes, swimming, cycling, or lifting weights.

Consider the boom of large, vibrant senior communities, such as The Villages (Florida) and any one of the many Del Webb communities located throughout North America. These are sprawling campuses that would dwarf even the largest university and they boast facilities of all kinds for active, engaged, and social seniors: golf courses, tennis centers, bowling alleys, health clubs, as well as a nearly unlimited number of classrooms and gathering places for clubs, hobby pursuits, and adult studies of every kind.

You hear of even more extreme examples of active seniors all the time. In the March 16, 2015, edition of the *Toronto Star*, it was reported that Georgina Harwood celebrated her 100th birthday with a skydive. Let's just say that again—a *skydive!* After landing, she said she was going to follow it up with a shark-cage dive the week after. For Harwood, a great-grandmother, this was her third skydive. She executed her first when she was ninety-two years old in 2007.

Jaring Timmerman, a record-breaking swimmer from Winnipeg, Manitoba, died at the age of 105. Only a year earlier he had set Masters world records in both the 50-meter freestyle and 50-meter backstroke events.

PBS NewsHour economics correspondent, Paul Solman, told the story in 2013 of Vita Needle, an eighty-year-old company in Needham, Massachusetts. The average age of workers at the family-owned needle and tube manufacturer is seventy-four years. At the time of the PBS feature, the oldest employee was Rosa Finnegan, age 100, followed by Bill Ferson, age 94. Bob O'Mara, 78 years old, is a retired engineer who had worked at Vita Needle for eleven years.

This is just a tiny sample of what some "elderly" individuals are doing today. The question we need to ask ourselves is whether these people really retired, because it's pretty evident that they have not withdrawn or retreated. And if they are not retired, what are they?

Retirement is still a perfectly good word, but we need to rein in its usage now that its original meaning is no longer all that relevant because people are living longer, healthier, more active lives. So the challenge now is to find a word that is more befitting to that period of time between when people leave their primary career and when they land in the proverbial rocking chair during their latter years.

FROM RETIREMENT TO VICTORY LAP: A NEW STAGE OF LIVING

In his highly influential book first published in 1978, *The Three Boxes of Life: And How to Get Out of Them*, Richard N. Bolles described three life stages: education, work, and retirement. Each of the three boxes Bolles described was a different size, relative to how the typical North American's life was structured at the time the book was written. The biggest box was the work stage and the smallest was the third, based on the old definition of retirement, comprising people lucky enough to reach the artificial retirement

finish line of 65 years old. The reward for getting to the retirement box was being able to sit back and watch the world go by for
a couple of years.

Lifeline

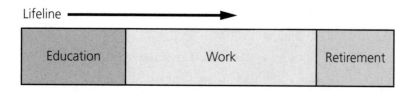

As stated earlier in the chapter, this framework for life worked
fine until people started to live longer. Instead of a retirement
stage lasting a few years, we are now looking at a stage that could
last as long as, or longer than, a person's work stage. We think
everyone would agree that's way too long to spend in a rocking
chair! And some might also argue thirty or forty years is a long
time to go without a paycheck.

To take into account the effect of increased longevity, it
makes sense to insert a new box before "retirement." We have
chosen to call this new third stage "Victory Lap," in recognition
of the increasingly common reality whereby individuals pursue
work with greater balance, meaning, and flexibility, even after
their core working years.

Lifeline

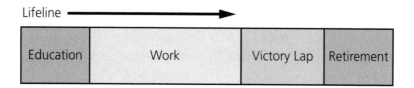

People entering the Victory Lap stage are at a point when many
of the primary responsibilities they once had have been eliminated or are down to greatly reduced and manageable levels. These
responsibilities include helping the kids finance post-secondary

education and leave home, eliminating all non–tax-deductible consumer debt (chiefly credit cards), and, ideally, paying off the mortgage. Achieving more financial independence gives people an opportunity to decide what to do with their newfound time and freedom. People now have options—options they haven't had for a very long time.

Having options is a wonderful thing. Options make life interesting and allow you to be creative again, and following through on options makes you happy! That's why we like to call this very active stage of "retirement" your Victory Lap. You've crossed the finish line and left the world of working-to-make-a-living behind. You've conquered many of the financial hurdles of your younger years, and now you can leave the rat race and follow a path of your own choosing.

In your Victory Lap, you continue to work, but you have the luxury of choosing to do only work that gives you what you want. Money and security are no longer the main motivators, because achieving financial independence has finally allowed you to make a change in your priorities. You can now work on your own terms. The opportunity is to design work to your liking, whether it be full-time or part-time. The central theme is a move towards balance, allowing you to pursue your personal goals (e.g., health, family, travel, hobbies) while earning an income as well. The key here is that in your Victory Lap you are still engaged: learning and growing, enjoying life to its fullest.

It's important for each of us to pause, reflect, and think about what it is we really want out of this stage of life. If we plan for it properly, this period of time could deliver more purpose and meaning than did our previous working life. We are not working for the love or need of money, we are working for the love of work because it feels good. We are not just working but, rather, living again.

The goal in stage three, the Victory Lap, is to extend this period of freedom, living like a kid again for as long as possible and squeezing every ounce out of life. Instrumental to doing so are these factors:

- maintaining your physical and mental health
- adopting a positive attitude
- ensuring that your financial plan is aligned with your life plan

After all is said and done, there will come a time when we will finally "retire" to the fourth and final life stage. No longer capable of being independent, we will become increasingly dependent on others for care and support during our remaining years. Many of us are going through this stage with our parents right now and are learning first-hand the realities and challenges of eldercare. Let's agree to confine our talk of "retirement" to the final, less vibrant stage of life. Our focus is on helping you to plan for the time prior to that final stage: a Victory Lap that's fulfilling, flexible, energizing—exactly what we all dream about and work so hard to achieve.

THE FUTURE OF RETIREMENT

The world of retirement is changing rapidly, like never before. Because people are living longer, with hundred-year lifespans becoming commonplace, this will have a huge impact on how we view work, education, and retirement in the years ahead—especially as people are not just living longer, they are also more active and vibrant in their later years than used to be typical.

When we began a search for Victory Lap role models, we bumped into the story of Professor Fred Kummerow, the driving force behind the fight to get trans fats out of our diets. After spending nearly sixty years writing about the link between trans fats and heart disease, and after starting a lawsuit against the U.S. Food and Drug Administration for failure to act upon his findings, Kummerow scored a major victory when the FDA made it a requirement for food companies to phase out the fats. Professor Kummerow officially retired from the University of Illinois at age seventy-one but never quit working. He maintained a lab at the university until he was 101, a year before his death in 2017, and he was riding a bike to get there every day well into his eighties.

So living longer is a good thing, right? Maybe. It all depends on how you define living. In the greater scheme of things, the key is to understand that the trend of increased longevity is going to have a huge and profoundly disruptive impact on retirement, social, and workplace norms; we need to find ways to adapt successfully to this new environment.

Most of our current retirement thinking and assumptions are based on information we inherited from the twentieth century, and these old assumptions do not reflect the current reality. If you were twenty-two in 1973, you could expect to live to age sixty-seven. But with life expectancy now past eighty for most North Americans, the math doesn't work anymore. The old formula of working like a dog from age twenty to age sixty-five, then enjoying a few years of a happy retirement, no longer works. (Did it ever really work at all?) The fact is that many people will need to work longer.

But the arithmetic is not the only concern, as living longer isn't fun if most of those extra years are spent in poor health. We believe people need to adapt to the new reality if they wish to maximize the quality of life in their latter years. Work—the *right* work, for which you have a passion and that you love to do—can enhance your life and keep you active and engaged for a good chunk of those extra years. This book is intended to help you find that type of work, and as much or as little of it as is right for you, so that you can enjoy all the other good things in life.

Given that you could have an extra thirty years of life after you exit your primary career, you can and should live life differently all the way through. You can exit the workforce more gradually, making the well-defined line between working and retirement a lot fuzzier—essentially mixing work and retirement for a long period of time. That is, in your working years you can enjoy some of what you would normally have put off for retirement; and when you normally would have retired, you can plan instead to enjoy a Victory Lap—with a little bit (or as much as you want) of work, and a lot of freedom to do and explore other things.

So as we say in our subtitle (*Work While You Play, Play While You Work*), in the Victory Lap the traditional distinction between work and leisure starts to fade. Increasingly, it becomes possible to structure our lives so that work often starts to resemble play and, as anyone who works at home well knows, play can often be interspersed with what we once would have considered "work."

WHY DO MEDIA SELL THE WRONG VERSION OF RETIREMENT?

Why does the advertising industry continue to sell us a version of retirement that doesn't reflect the current reality? For some strange reason, the financial media and financial services industries have not adjusted their traditional view of retirement to take into account the increased life expectancy and the changing demographics we've been describing. While this is puzzling, bankers are pretty smart, so surely they have a good reason for it. Or maybe their focus is on other things. Whatever the reason, they continue to sell the dream whereby, after working for several decades, one can finally enjoy a retirement that is filled with leisure and consumption.

You know the images, the ones that can be found in every second "retirement" advertisement: seemingly carefree, happy couples sitting on a beach in the Caribbean while sipping on a strawberry daiquiri; or perhaps they're sailing on a yacht, with the sun shining and the wind blowing through their hair as they embrace each other, smiling. Everything is perfect, perfect, perfect! And all of this could be yours if you only start saving a small amount of money each month. Or how about the other common image, in which a happy couple is playing golf on a picturesque course beside the ocean? You can almost hear the sound of the putt going into the hole for a birdie.

But when you stop to think about it, spending your next twenty years on a beach, a yacht, or a golf course is very expensive and probably out of reach for a lot of people, especially so for those who have raised kids. According to *MoneySense* magazine, the average cost of raising a child to age eighteen in Canada is a whopping $243,660. That's $12,825 per child per year or $1,070 per month. And that's before you send them off to college or university!

Because the reality for most of us doesn't match what advertisers are telling us our "retirement" years should look like, it can cause us to feel anxiety and discouragement from knowing in our hearts that the vision is likely out of reach. The financial services industry doesn't help matters much either, as it creates the fear that we will not have enough in retirement to enjoy what they tell us we all deserve: the big house or vacation property, an expensive golf course membership, luxury cars, and exotic trips around the world. People who are trying to get us to buy their products or services have a tendency to make us feel we are not good enough unless we buy what the beautiful people are buying. They cast a

"My Father told me that whoever dies with the most toys, wins."

spell, making us feel that something is always missing and that if we just had that one last thing everything would be okay.

That kind of thinking is just plain wrong. And wait, it gets worse, because even if you can afford the dream, odds are that, over time, you will become bored and disillusioned by it because it was never *your* dream—it was always *their* dream, planted in your mind! Truth be told, only a small portion of people identify with the idea of golfing or sailing in their later years, so the question should be, why do the retirement ads not reflect the current reality of retirement? The answer is simple: reality doesn't sell! Picture an ad depicting a gray-haired couple living in a small bungalow, each sitting in a different room. She's watching *The Price Is Right* and he's watching *Seinfeld* reruns on Netflix. The advertisement that shows them having dinner at Olive Garden or Denny's a couple of times a month just doesn't seem very glamorous, but it is the reality for many.

We believe that if you focus on designing the Victory Lap that's right for you, you can avoid falling prey to the advertisers' spell, thereby preventing yourself from feeling inadequate or frustrated if you can't attain what they think you should want, and avoiding the life of penury and boredom to which many who lead a passive retirement are resigned. Somewhere between these two extremes you can plan and live the life beyond traditional work that *you* want.

MIKE ON BOREDOM

I remember when my family moved to a different part of the city when I was fifteen. There I was, at the beginning of summer, in a strange place with no friends and nothing to do, because I had missed the deadline for registration for baseball and other organized summer activities. So I spent the entire summer watching TV.

Eventually I became so in tune with the program schedules that I was able to tell the time of day or night by what show was on. Days drifted into weeks, weeks into months, and thankfully it was soon time to get back to school. How many kids do you know who are happy to go back to school? That's what boredom does to you!

It was a wasted summer, but it served me well because it provided a good taste of what real, sustained boredom is like. Boredom eats at your soul, and prolonged exposure to television actually has a numbing effect. After experiencing that, I made a promise to myself that I would never allow myself to go through another period like it again.

BOREDOM IN RETIREMENT: THE ELEPHANT IN THE ROOM

Unfortunately, for many people retirement is not much different from Mike's summer of endless TV watching, but for them the boredom lasts for years, not weeks and months, and it can literally be a killer. We all know by now the health benefits of an active lifestyle and, conversely, that a sedentary life increases health risks and takes years off your life—so yes, you really can die of boredom. When you think about the fact that many people spend some of what could be their best years watching TV because they can't afford to do something else or, worse, they can't think of anything else to do, it's hard not to get a little angry because we're doing this to ourselves; we are slowly dying inside if we choose a life of boredom.

There's no question that boredom isn't reserved only for people who can't afford to do other things. The reality is that any retirement based solely on one kind of activity—whether it be sitting on a beach somewhere drinking margaritas or golfing all day—usually ends in boredom. People need to be challenged constantly, and not just by who hits the longest drive. For this reason, boredom can be a living hell, no matter how much or how little that boring lifestyle costs.

Even in retirement you still need to get up each day, put clothes on, and find interesting, satisfying, and meaningful activities to fill the day. This period of your life could potentially last longer than the entire time you spent working, so you'd better think of some good ways to make your days challenging, stimulating, and rewarding. In chapter 3 we will help you find your *ikigai*, your reason to get out of bed in the morning.

A common misconception is that retirement is some Holy Grail whereby those who reach it become instantly happy and finally start enjoying life more. The truth is that if you weren't happy *before* retirement, the odds are that your life will not change much *in* retirement, and it could even turn out to be worse. The key for a happy retirement is to stay engaged, set challenging goals, and continue to take risks. For the co-authors of this book, continuing to work to some degree is important for our happiness. It keeps us busy and provides the fun money we need to finance the many adventures we've planned for our own Victory Laps.

ROB ON BOREDOM

I remember a number of years ago playing a round of golf with a colleague and a couple of his friends, John and Tony, at their private club. The friends were both fully retired in their early sixties. They were part of a social group that had all sold their businesses or left corporate work in their late fifties with enough money to be retired. After having a post-round beer, we got up from our chairs and said our goodbyes. As we parted, I recall John turned to Tony and said, "Are you coming back to play cards tonight?" Tony responded by saying, "Of course, what else would I do?"

That small comment really struck me. Tony appeared to have so little going on that he seemed resigned to his schedule. Presumably, the only reason he was coming back to the club to play cards with his friends was the absence of anything else even remotely engaging enough to capture his attention. I remember thinking at the time, what a shame and how sad for Tony. It is one of the first times I can recall thinking about the dangers of retirement: the potential for the malaise of too much time and not enough meaningful activity to keep one engaged and passionate about life. Here was an individual who was financially secure enough to belong to a wonderful private club and have good friends to spend time with. Still, his life had become stale, rote.

That short conversation has stayed with me over the years as I have worked with many clients planning their own retirement. We always say that people need to have something to retire *to*. We can't just retire *from* work and not find something else to replace it. We need purpose and passion to really enjoy each day. Ironically, in the years following that round of golf, I heard through my colleague that most of the members of that social group had ultimately returned to work. Absent a better option, it seems that they each had decided that the merits of work (compensation, social interaction, challenge, etc.) outweighed the boredom of their early retirement.

WHY STOP WORKING? IT MIGHT KILL YOU!

Retirement kills more people than hard work ever did.

—*Malcolm Forbes*

Most people say when you get old you have to give things up, but I think we get old because we give things up.

—*Former U.S. Senator Theodore Green (who was ninety-eight when he retired in 1966!)*

Many people are starting to wake up and are realizing that the old version of retirement—saving for thirty years or more to fund a remaining period of leisure—just doesn't work for them. They are coming to understand that life was not meant to be a spectator sport and that watching TV for hours on end just won't cut it, especially as the average lifespan is increasing. People are concerned with how they are going to fill their days while they are still feeling healthy and active. How will they be able to afford such a long period of retirement? How can they maintain a satisfying and stress-free life? Folks are beginning to understand there is still so much more they can get out of life and that continuing to work in some capacity can play a big part in this.

While "retirees" may want to stay in the game workwise, they can now call the shots and do it on their own terms. They have finally reached a time when they are able to view work differently and they are no longer working solely because they need the money. This time around they are doing work for the sheer joy of it and because it gives them a reason to get out of bed with a smile each morning.

ROB ON *REAL* RETIREMENT GOALS

In my planning practice, we note very specifically the words clients use to describe their financial goals. As words are windows to the soul, we make sure to capture and use the exact phrasing our clients use to articulate what compels them.

Recently we surveyed a cross section of client goals and noticed some interesting patterns. The words and phrases that appeared most were around concepts like "flexibility," "choice," and "control." People seem to want similar versions of the same thing: greater balance and freedom.

Notice that freedom and balance aren't necessarily the same thing as the freedom defined by our traditional view of the full-stop retirement. I have come to believe that rather than not working at all, what most people really want to do is to work on their own terms.

The thing is, once you have achieved some degree of financial independence, work *feels* different. You may have noticed that those who have achieved greater financial freedom are the fun people to hang out with—they have a certain joie de vivre that can only come from working not because they *have* to but because they *want* to. They are doing things that may look like work to casual observers but to them really isn't. That's because the meaning of work is reversed for people who choose to remain active and engaged: they are accomplishing something that matters to them, and the financial reward is a happy by-product. Once you take the *need* for money out of the equation, work can be a wonderful source of happiness and freedom.

We believe that when people choose to delay total retirement and instead continue to work in a job that they enjoy, on their own terms, they reap several benefits:

1. **Delaying retirement reduces financial anxiety.**
    The greatest fear many have is outliving their money. People are losing sleep over rising health-care costs and the erosive effects of inflation. Postponing full retirement allows you to consider delaying when you start to receive government benefits, which will pay off greatly down the road. For example, in Canada if you delayed taking Canada Pension Plan (CPP) benefits to age seventy you would receive 42 percent more than if you had taken it at sixty-five, and a similar dynamic is at work with Social Security in the United States. Prolonging the amount of time you earn employment income of some kind will also allow you to continue to save for the future and probably delay drawing from your retirement savings, and you'll be better able to finance your desired lifestyle in the meantime.

2. **Delaying retirement will help you live longer.**
   Numerous studies have shown that mortality rates
   improve with an older retirement age. A ninety-year
   study of 1,528 Americans called *The Longevity Project*
   showed that people who chose to delay retirement
   had much longer lives than their retired, golfing
   counterparts. The continually productive men and
   women lived significantly longer than their couch-
   sitting, TV-watching friends. "It wasn't the happiest
   or the most relaxed older participants who lived the
   longest," the authors wrote, "it was those who were
   most engaged in pursuing their goals." The evidence is
   clear: having a purpose, a reason for getting out of bed
   in the morning, knowing where you are going and being
   committed to, and focused on, getting there is going to
   make you live longer.

3. **Delaying retirement will keep you healthier for
   longer.**
   Staying in the work game keeps you vital, involved,
   and healthier because you have to use your mind and
   body in order to work. Retiring early only increases the
   chances of entering a long period of intellectual atrophy
   and monotonous leisure.

4. **Delaying retirement will insulate you from
   boredom.**
   Boredom is dangerous, as it can lead to self-destructive
   behavior that accelerates the aging process and increases
   the odds of a person having a short and unhappy
   retirement. Why spend all those years saving up for a
   long retirement, only to end up killing yourself through

your behavior? Don't settle for watching *Seinfeld* reruns all day when you are capable of so much more.

BEWARE OF SUDDEN RETIREMENT SYNDROME

Relatively soon, I will die. Maybe in twenty years, maybe tomorrow, it doesn't matter. Once I am dead and everyone who knows me dies too, it will be as though I never existed. What difference has my life made to anyone? None that I can think of. None at all.

—*From the movie* About Schmidt

As far as we know, sudden retirement syndrome is not a real medical condition, but it does describe the shock of withdrawal that can occur when a person suddenly ends their career. Sudden retirement syndrome can be brought on by downsizing, formal retirement, and other events; but no matter the cause, the shock of going unprepared from being engaged in a busy work life to doing absolutely nothing can be very stressful, fraught with risks, and in extreme cases can even result in premature death. We have all heard stories of people in retirement who lost their motivation to do much of anything, started drinking heavily, for example, and died soon after.

Deciding to retire (or having your company or manager make that decision for you) is one of the single biggest life changes a person can go through. When you think about it, it is a kind of loss. It could be a happy loss or a sad loss, but to be suddenly without something to which you devoted so much of your life can result in a profound, personal inner loss. For some it will feel like a death of sorts: death of one's corporate identity.

Truth be told, retirement shock can be hell for many. You start to feel alone as the stress and anxiety build; no one seems to understand what you are going through. Most of the people in your life can't help because they can't relate to you being unhappy that you don't have to go to work anymore. It just doesn't make sense to them.

Usually stress can be alleviated by removing external stressors, like a bad boss or excessive demands at work, but with sudden retirement syndrome there is no external stressor to remove, as the stress comes from within ourselves. And if we cannot find a way to manage this stress, depression will eventually set in, and depression is a very bad thing. It robs you of your energy, vitality, and self-esteem, and generally leads to poor health. With depression typically come an unrelenting sad mood, an absence of energy, problems of concentrating or remembering, a loss of interest in activities previously enjoyed, and difficulties with sleeping and eating.

Not everyone will experience sudden retirement syndrome, but for those who do it can be mitigated by a person's degree of preparedness. People need to be aware of the emotional challenges they are likely to face and prepare themselves, both financially and psychologically, for the unexpected. Essentially, what each person needs to do is create and maintain his or her own version of an escape pod in case of emergency—and this is where Victory Lap thinking comes in. There will always be some anxiety involved in leaving the Corp, but it will be much less stressful if you view leaving as an opportunity to be free again; to find new purpose and rebuild yourself. If you are able to find something that can replace the loss, something that gets you excited, odds are you will find this period in your life to be one of the happiest.

WOULD WE BE SO OBSESSED WITH RETIRING IF WE ENJOYED OUR JOBS?

Consider the following headline: *Gallup Poll: 70% of Americans Hate Their Stupid Jobs*. The article described a Gallup 2013 State of the American Workplace study in which 70 percent of those who participated described themselves as "disengaged" from their work. It's sad, isn't it, to think of so many people working in jobs they hate? No wonder the fantasy of complete retirement looks so appealing to so many. You can see why people convince themselves that the only answer is to grin and bear it until they have the opportunity to retire and leave that job they loathe once and for all.

So many of us bought into the idea that we need to sacrifice a good portion of our lives and chase after money so we can one day achieve security for the family. We held this belief for decades, in part a reflection of a good old-fashioned work ethic, in part a concession to the practical responsibilities of being spouses and parents. But it's crazy to keep doing something you hate (or even merely dislike) just so you can eventually accumulate enough money to finally do what it is you really enjoy doing. The stress could end up killing you before you have a chance to enjoy the money for which you spent so many years working.

In 2014, findings were reported by Statistics Canada, which had followed a group of workers who were aged fifty to sixty-four when they left their jobs. Ten years later, most had gone back to work; just 32 percent of the men and 36 percent of the women had not. Among those who left their careers in their early sixties, the agency found that 47 percent of the men and 41 percent of the women were re-employed within the next ten years, and most had rejoined the workforce within a year or two.

Based on these findings, one might conclude that in all probability many of the workers had jumped into early retirement to escape a job they disliked. However, once retired the participants discovered that they needed more: not just more money, but also the social interaction, structure, and feeling of accomplishment and purpose that the workplace can provide.

The truth is, most of us would not be obsessed with retiring if we had a job that we truly enjoyed and that we were doing for the right reasons. We need to stop complaining about how unhappy we are and instead focus on how we can find something we have always wanted to do, and do it on our own terms. How can we invest our time, energy, and money to create the lifestyle that we have always wanted? This is what each of us must determine for ourselves.

• • •

It's clear that the traditional full-stop retirement model just doesn't work anymore. While it's good news that we will be living longer, this poses the challenge of figuring out how to make sure that those additional years are well spent with minimal stress and maximum satisfaction. Adopting a Victory Lap lifestyle will help you to ensure that your later years are satisfying ones, because in Victory Lap you are no longer defined by what you once did, instead you become who you once were. It allows you to get back that carefree feeling of your youth while at the same time benefiting from the wisdom gained over a lifetime of experiences. This book was written for the people who want more out of life, those who want to spend the rest of their lives making great memories while squeezing as much life as possible out of their remaining years.

2

Welcome to the Corporate Jungle

Every morning in Africa, a gazelle wakes up. It knows that it must run faster than the fastest lion, or it will be killed. Every morning a lion wakes up. It knows that it must outrun the slowest gazelle, or it will starve to death. It doesn't matter whether you are a lion or a gazelle: when the sun comes up, you better be running.
—African parable

There is something very wrong with the work world today: it is far too common to find employees who are tired, over-worked, stressed out, and living in fear of an uncertain future. As a result, people are eating too much, watching too much television, and complaining too much, often self-medicating with drugs and/or alcohol or taking prescription medication to cope with their distress. How can it be that in North America, one of the most prosperous societies in the world, people are taking more medications for anxiety, depression, and sleep disorders than ever before?

As a population we are out of balance; our quality of life is being adversely affected and work is playing a significant role in what is happening. The societal norm is to focus on developing a career and becoming prosperous at the expense of everything else, even our families and our health. We have become consumed by work.

STARTING ON THE WRONG FOOT

Throughout most of our lives we are told what to do, and therein lies the problem. It begins with the direction given to us by the education system and our parents. We are taught from an early age that the purpose of working hard and getting good grades is so that we will be able to get a good job that pays lots of money. With few exceptions, everything we were told was linked to the future and the goal of making more money. This is dangerous thinking, as you end up always trying to get somewhere other than where you are, forever chasing more money. You are never truly satisfied, as you are always focused on becoming, achieving, and attaining. This way of thinking creates stress, and stress over a prolonged period is harmful to our minds and bodies.

When a person starts a corporate career, he or she makes a deal with the Corp, trading personal freedom and dreams for money and the promise of security. The Corp says, "Do what you are told and work hard, and we will provide you and your family with a good living. If you continue to play ball and be a good soldier, in forty years you will retire with an excellent pension and a beautiful home fully paid for."

The corporate world's definition of success is programmed into our heads from day one, and it's fueled by the continual enticement of wealth, status, and the accumulation of material goods. We were taught the importance of following our bosses' orders; if we conformed and became a productive part of the organization, we were rewarded with prizes and shiny trinkets (which, in Mike's case, now fill up a significant part of his garage). The lure of these trinkets and prizes causes us to forget that true happiness is derived from achieving our dreams, attaining our personal goals, and having a loving family.

For those of us who accepted the corporate agreement, for a period of time everything worked out the way it was supposed to. But the Corp demanded a high price for its promises of safety and wealth. It demanded that we give up who we were, become compliant and obedient, and accept its version of the dream. We kept our part of the bargain for as long as we could, but eventually people's needs change and some of us can't keep the bargain any more. Blame it on Maslow.

MASLOW AND THE CORPORATE WORLD

If you plan on being anything less than you are capable of being,
you will probably be unhappy all the days of your life.
—Abraham Maslow

Abraham Maslow was a psychologist who published a seminal paper in 1943 called "A Theory of Human Motivation." Maslow believed people are motivated to take care of certain needs and that when one need is fulfilled a person seeks to fulfill the next one, and so on. His famous "hierarchy of needs" theory consists of the following five levels:

1. Physiological needs: food, water, shelter, sleep
2. Safety needs: protection from the elements, security, stability, protection from danger
3. Love and belongingness needs: friendship, camaraderie, love, affection
4. Esteem needs: achievement, mastery, status, dominance, prestige, self-respect, respect from others
5. Self-actualization needs: realizing personal potential, self-fulfillment, seeking personal growth and peak experiences, helping others, sensing that you are doing what you are most fitted for

Once the first four levels are satisfied, Maslow theorized, those needs would no longer have the power to motivate us and people would feel discontented unless they experienced self-actualization or, as we like to call it, self-intentionalization.

Throughout our university years, we tend to rank high on the Maslow scale. Our physiological needs are being met: we have food and shelter, whether we are living in residence or are still in the family home. Our self-esteem needs are being met, as at this point in our lives the world is full of possibilities and we feel good about ourselves and our future.

During those early years, according to Maslow, we would rank just below the self-actualization level. But things change after you move out of the house, land a corporate job, and start your own family. Suddenly you find yourself near the bottom of the Maslow scale: most of your attention becomes focused on protecting your family, paying off the mortgage, and saving for eventual retirement.

When you join a corporation you are, in effect, making an informal agreement that you are willing to give over your life to the Corp in exchange for security for your family. It sounds harsh, but that's the reality for most of us. Many of us are wired to succeed, win awards, and earn promotions. The pressure to produce outstanding individual performance in a competitive environment leads to long hours and hard work. As a result, we end up spending most of our time at work or thinking about work. In doing so, we sacrifice our personal freedom to be who we really are. Indeed, some people so strongly identify with the Corp that the corporate roles they play can take over and essentially become who they are, and not being true to your own nature is not healthy in the long run.

THE TRAP

While it's possible for people at all levels within the Corp to feel a significant measure of mastery, fulfillment, personal growth, and self-fulfillment—those higher-level needs that Maslow talked about—the trade-off is that we often have a financial dependency on the Corp. This dependency is exacerbated by the rising costs

Ed's ball got a lot larger after he
bought the bigger house in the suburbs...

of family life in the form of mortgages, cars, clothes, and kids. At a certain point we are driven into complete economic dependency through debt, new family needs, and consumerism.

This is when the fear starts to creep in. Salaries and bonuses may keep rising, but lifestyle inflation outpaces them, resulting in more consumption and more debt. That deepens the dependency, which then deepens the fear of job loss. It's a vicious circle, and before you know it you're trapped. You essentially give up your personal freedom in exchange for economic security, which is not even guaranteed. One day you realize the rules have changed and that working for the Corp is no longer a safe bet: people are in full-blown survivor mode trying to navigate the now-commonplace restructurings, downsizing, and mergers. Even long-term boomer employees and those with outstanding track records can end up on the chopping block. "That's business," as corporate bosses are fond of saying.

Even if you do reach a point when you start to feel financially secure, at the same time you might realize that your career no longer delivers the meaning you thought it would. Yet you spend your precious time working at a job that no longer excites you, with people you don't care much about, all for the sake of a little more money, and it causes you to die a little bit each day. You find yourself sitting at work, glancing now and then at your pension statement, trying to hang on so that you can maximize your payout and then finally begin enjoying life.

Perhaps you allowed yourself to be seduced and sucked into someone else's definition of success, until the day you wake up and think to yourself, "Hey, what happened to my life? It wasn't supposed to be this way!" While your material standard of living may be at an all-time high, your quality of life may be at an all-time low.

Why do so many of us decide to stay with the Corp, remain unhappy, and go on suffering? Well, by this point in our lives we have invested so much time and energy chasing financial security that it's hard to take a different tack and try something else. Learning to do something new later in life is just too scary for a lot of people: we often lack the confidence in ourselves to succeed; the perceived risk is just too great. People reason to themselves, why walk away from the twenty years that were invested in the Corp? But we think the real question should be, why waste the *next* twenty years doing something you dislike?

Job intensity has ramped up over the years, and today it seems like most people are just trying to find ways to keep up the pace. Years ago, jobs in most corporations had built-in seasonality; there was some downtime at some point. Today, however, it's pedal to the metal and business lulls are a thing of the past; managers track your sales results hourly, and every day is a competition with your co-workers. It reminds us of the oft-cited imagery of frogs in a pot of water on a stove, and in this case it is management that's turning up the temperature slowly so that nobody notices how hot it is until it's too late.

We end up going home at the end of the workday physically
and mentally drained, with nothing left to give to our families.
The best part of our day often consists of sitting down in front of
the TV, rewarding ourselves with snacks and a drink (or three)
for having survived another day. No matter how much money we
make, status we have earned, or power we hold, we have allowed
ourselves to become prisoners of the corporate institution.

The concept of institutionalism is well-defined in the movie
The Shawshank Redemption (adapted from the novella written by
Stephen King), which depicts life in a federal prison in the 1940s
and '50s. As it's portrayed, the system was designed to stamp out
any hope of freedom for its prisoners. The character Red, who's
played by Morgan Freeman, has some particularly insightful
lines about what it means to be institutionalized:

> *These walls are funny. First you hate 'em, then you get used to*
> *'em. Enough time passes, you get so you depend on them. That's*
> *institutionalized. They send you here for life, that's exactly*
> *what they take. The part that counts anyway.*

The effects of incarceration on Shawshank Prison's long-term
inmates are not unlike the effects of working in the corporate
world, which is an institution in itself. Early in the movie, Brooks,
who was a prisoner for over fifty years, discovers he will soon be
set free; however, because he is so accustomed to the routines that
have been long established for him, rather than be thrilled by
this news, he's haunted by the realization that he will be unable
to function in the real world and survive. As Red put it, "In here
he's somebody, out there he's nobody." Soon after being released,
Brooks commits suicide because he is unable to cope with change
and life outside the prison institution.

Another prisoner, Andy, recognizes early on the importance of remaining tied to his life outside the walls, to have hope and to live for something, or else life isn't worth living. Andy refuses to sit in his cell for eighty years and wait to die. The hope of one day returning to the outside world is what motivates him to spend twenty years digging a tunnel to escape by crawling through a septic pipe.

START DIGGING YOUR ESCAPE TUNNEL

When you think about it in broader terms, you can see how the Corp can institutionalize you just as surely as Shawshank Prison did its inmates—but only if you allow it to. The smart ones among us do as Andy does and start digging their escape tunnel toward freedom (financial independence) the minute they join the Corp. They view the time they spend in the Corp as part of a bigger plan, adopting the institution purposefully and using the benefits it provides to help them reach their long-term goals.

Working toward financial independence and an eventual Victory Lap will give you hope and comfort, secure in the knowledge that you will one day get back control over your life, your future, and your time. Instead of focusing on how the Corp uses you, look at it in a different fashion: How are you using the Corp to meet your goals of financial independence ?

If you haven't already started, you need to begin planning today for your "jailbreak" by creating your own destiny and charting your eventual Victory Lap. You really don't have another choice if you want to stay sane. It's crazy to stay in a job that no longer satisfies you, forever living with the fear of one day being forced out and being replaced by a younger, cheaper model.

ROB ON THE TUNNEL TO TEACHING

A very good friend of mine spent his entire career in corporate marketing, mostly for global food companies. He started building his escape tunnel quite early. During his forties, Eric was fortunate to be on some senior executive teams. "I noticed that no one on the team had gray hair," Eric likes to say. That, to him, was an epiphany. He realized in those boardrooms that the corporate world drives everyone away at some point. There's not a lot of folks "dying with their boots on" in Fortune 500–size companies. As a result, Eric started to dig his escape tunnel.

Always the mentor and coach, Eric felt his calling for his next chapter was teaching. He approached a friend at a prestigious local university for advice on how to break into the college arena as a business professor. Eric's friend suggested he cut his teeth at the community college level. With approval from his employer, Eric began teaching night classes on the side in his mid-fifties. After a few years refining his curriculum and approach, he got a tryout at the university level. After a couple of semesters, his classes were so popular there was a waiting list. He expanded from there into running executive programs and corporate engagements for the university, ultimately parlaying that into numerous corporate consulting engagements. Eric once told me, "I make a fraction of what I made in corporate America, but I have more professional growth opportunities and more time in my life."

It's been ten years and Eric's not slowing down at all. Why would he? He arranges his schedule with periods of intense work and focus followed by extended breaks. I love it when I email him during one of those break periods. I get a quick auto-reply from him saying, "I am off the grid," and promising that he won't be checking or returning any messages until he returns. After decades in the corporate environs working long hours, traveling almost constantly around the globe, he's now created a balanced existence of work, family, and fun!

HAVE YOU SERVED YOUR TIME?

It just doesn't stand to reason: why would you do stuff you don't like for more than thirty years, just so you can cash in on a pension or your retirement savings at the end? (And that's assuming you even make it to the end.) After a certain point, you must decide whether to keep your head down for a few more years in a job you hate or that's killing you with stress, or take a pay cut to work at something you could love doing for the rest of your days. Staying with the Corp and continuing to save for a supposedly successful retirement, primarily for the sake of buying more things, doesn't make sense if the prolonged stress of your job could cut your retirement life in half.

It's hard to understand why people feel they need to remain in prison even though the door is unlocked. Brooks had no choice, but we do, so why do so many of us choose to be imprisoned by our work? Problems arise when we stop putting our whole heart into life. The moment boredom rules our life, something dies within us. But despite unhappy circumstances, people rarely take the initiative to change their situation. Over the years they become conditioned to a life of security and conformity. This may appear to provide peace of mind, but in reality nothing is more damaging to a person's present quality of life than a secure future. The core of a person's spirit is passion for adventure. The joy of life comes from our encounters with new experiences, so it's important to accept change as a key part of our lives. Don't let your life spark be extinguished. Disengaged employees who waste their lives in unenjoyable dead-end jobs aren't making a living, they're making a dying!

Understand at the outset that the role of the Corp is to serve as a stepping stone to achieving the goal of financial freedom, and once you reach that goal your shackles will no longer exist. You will be free to decide whether to stay with the Corp or leave and create a Victory Lap lifestyle that is more meaningful and that will deliver on all your higher-level needs. It is a decision that can be in your control and on your terms if you have first attained financial independence. We'll discuss how to determine how close you are to financial independence, starting in the next chapter.

Leaving a high-paying job late in life is a risk, no question; but staying in a job you detest and hanging on to the end is a far bigger risk. We can't guarantee that opting to do a Victory Lap will be painless, but we *can* guarantee that it'll be less painful than regretting what might have happened if you had only taken the chance to make a change when the opportunity was there.

It's always easy to find a reason to stay put, do nothing, and not take a risk. So decide in advance, right now, to quit your present job someday. Create your exit plan for the day you will stop working for someone else and begin working for yourself. Make a list of what you'll need to do in order to make it happen—to break out of the Corp and start your own version of a Victory Lap, which will allow you to find happiness, fulfillment, and security on your own terms (if you are interested in help developing your to-do list see chapter 6). Believe in yourself and know that you are smart enough, talented enough, and motivated enough to succeed in this crucial new stage of your life. Reduce your material needs and adopt a more frugal lifestyle. Get healthy. Start now!

• • •

For the record, we do not want to appear overly negative about working in the corporate world. When we set out to write this chapter, we were so focused on warning people about the dangers of working in the corporate jungle that we initially ignored many of the positive benefits that Corps can provide.

For example, Mike and Jonathan both agree that, looking back at their own multi-decade corporate careers, work was fun for a while and they were both good at it. They both earned good money, which helped them achieve many of their goals. Rob sees these benefits, too, with many of his clients who work for the Corp; they are able to pay off the mortgage, raise the kids, help pay for their education, and achieve financial independence. Mike even had the added fortune of meeting his wife (whom he affectionately calls "the Contessa") at work, so you could say working at a Corp paid off in more ways than one for him. But like everything in life, the benefits of working in an organization come at a cost. It's this cost that we feel most people are not truly aware of, and that's why we felt we needed to point it out.

So let's say it again: it's crazy to work in a job you no longer enjoy just so you can save more money for a retirement about which you have no idea. You need to create a long-term plan and design a Victory Lap that will deliver to you the lifestyle that you always dreamed about. The rest of the book is designed to help you do exactly that.

3

Victory Lap Retirement

It's Never Too Late to Find Your Purpose

A master in the art of living draws no sharp distinction between his work and his play, his labor and his leisure, his mind and his body, his education and his recreation. He hardly knows which is which. He simply pursues his vision of excellence through whatever he is doing and leaves others to determine whether he is working or playing. To him, he is always doing both.
　—*Lawrence Pearsall Jacks*

LESSONS FROM OKINAWA

Okinawa is a chain of islands off the coast of Japan and is home to some of the healthiest seniors on the planet, with many living past the century mark. Not only are these seniors among the longest-lived in the world, they also benefit from more healthy years, free from disability and illness. Heart disease and dementia rates are lower than average, and rates for breast and prostate cancer are even lower still. Obviously the elders of Okinawa are doing something right! Being smart people, why wouldn't we try to copy what they are doing?

In chapter 1 we described how in North America the concept of retirement evolved during the industrialization of the continent. Prior to that, most people lived on farms and farmers didn't retire. This is very similar to the thinking among Okinawan people, who refuse to believe in the concept of retirement and do not practice it. It's interesting to note that in the Okinawan language there isn't even a word for retirement. In its place is the term *ikigai* (eek-y-guy), which roughly translated means, "the reason for which you wake up in the morning."

Ikigai really means having a sense of purpose. There is a great deal of literature supporting the idea that people who have a strong sense of purpose are healthier and better able to deal with the difficulties that life may occasionally throw their way. Older Okinawans can readily articulate the reason why they get up in the morning. They live intentional, purposeful lives. They feel needed, they matter, they contribute, and as a result they live longer than most.

Once you have found your *ikigai*, why would you ever want to retire? What would you wish to retire to? People need a reason to live, and continuing to work at something they find enjoyable gives them that reason. Why would they ever want to take it away from themselves via retirement?

VICTORY LAP LIFESTYLE

In his book *The Blue Zones: Lessons for Living Longer from the People Who've Lived the Longest*, Dan Buettner clearly demonstrates how lifestyle choices are the key to a healthy and active old age. This is evidenced by the younger people of Okinawa who are seduced by the lure of high-paying jobs in high-stress environments, have poor diets, and don't get enough exercise. As a result, they are succumbing to the illnesses (heart disease, stroke, cancer, etc.) that the elders have managed to avoid. The younger people want more and they want it now, but the chase for more is killing them.

This kind of mentality is more in keeping with another Japanese word, one that is decidedly more ominous: *karoshi*, which means "death from overwork," caused by a lack of work-life balance. Sounds like we might be suffering from a little *karoshi* here in North America as well—working flat out for decades to attain the dream of a full-stop retirement that we may never live to see. Do you think maybe we have got this retirement thing all wrong? We sure think so.

After reviewing much of the prevailing retirement literature and longevity studies, we have concluded that for most of us a full-stop retirement is not the best way to go. People need to stop spending so much time worrying about making more money and worrying about retirement. Instead we should be focusing our efforts on making a great life while we still have the time. We need to work on optimizing our lifestyle with the goal of maximizing our life expectancy and the overall quality of our remaining years. We hate to break it to you, but sitting on a beach all day drinking piña coladas just isn't going to do it for you after a week or two.

In fact, a study published in 2005 that looked at Shell Oil employees in the United States showed that people who retired at age fifty-five were 89 percent more likely to die in the ten years after retirement than those who retired at sixty-five. The same study found that the workers who continued working to the age of sixty-five were 89 percent more likely to live ten more years after retirement even though they were ten years older than their early-retirement counterparts.

These findings suggest that, without a purpose, without a reason to get out of bed in the morning, people tend to live shorter lives. For many of us, work is our purpose and so when we retire we are in fact retiring from our purpose. Without purpose, we do not have a good reason to live, which is a sad way to go through the rest of your life. It's also important to note that just because you have achieved financial independence, it does not automatically mean that you will be living a fulfilling life. A life without purpose even if you have a lot of money is a sad life indeed.

The aforementioned Shell Oil employees and the elders in Okinawa are just a few examples of numerous longevity studies that have had similar findings, and the lessons they teach us are reflected in the new lifestyle philosophy of Victory Lap. The goal in Victory Lap is a re-balancing of leisure and work in a person's life in order to create a vibrant, healthy, low-stress, sustainable lifestyle.

The key is to slow down the pace of your life, even in the working years (which in turn will lower stress and anxiety), and to stay engaged and active later in life than the traditional full-stop retirement might allow. As we say in the subtitle of this book, we all need to learn to play a little more while we are working, and continue working to some degree while we are playing. This redistribution of work and leisure is a true work-life balance and is much healthier all around than the old slave-and-save retirement model.

We all must stop spending so much time chasing the big expensive pleasures in life; instead, we need to learn to enjoy the many little pleasures we often miss when we're wrapped up in our busy business lives. By slowing down you begin to see and appreciate things as if for the first time. You begin to live a more fulfilled life because you finally realize you are satisfied with where you are—you don't need to keep chasing more. Or as retirement expert Doug Dahmer puts it, you've reached the "Work Optional" stage. You finally understand that you have enough money to get by and that there are other, far better, reasons to get out of bed in the morning.

START PLANNING YOUR VICTORY LAP NOW

Smart Victory Lappers plan their exit from the corporate world well in advance. They view their corporate jobs as stepping stones toward the time when they won't have to worry about impressing the boss anymore and they will no longer have to endure time-sucking commutes, job plateauing, office politics, endless meetings, and pressured sales just for the money. And when they get to that point of financial independence, they don't wait for permission from someone to say it's okay for them to leave their primary job to start their Victory Lap: it was their plan all along.

By thinking this way and planning ahead, you will have a second chance in Victory Lap, and this time you'll get to connect the dots your way. Realize that most of your major responsibilities are now behind you, such as raising and educating the kids, paying down the mortgage, and so on. No matter what happens, you and your family will survive. So stop putting things off till tomorrow, because tomorrow you could be suffering from a life-changing illness. Never assume that opportunities that are available to you today will be available to you five years from now. Stuff happens! Be intentional with your remaining years, create and start living a wonderful life now!

When you think about it, Victory Lap is like a second childhood, where you use your additional years of salary or self-employment income to create new adventures and experiences. Remember back to how we lived when we were young adults. We didn't have a lot of money, but we always seemed to have just enough. We had the ability to eat what we wanted, live where we wanted, travel where we wanted, and we were free from anxiety and fear because everything seemed possible in our minds. We tended to live in the moment and didn't spend a lot of time and energy worrying about what happened yesterday or what tomorrow might bring. In Victory Lap we can start living like kids again, full of life and excitement.

THE BENEFITS OF A VICTORY LAP

There are countless benefits for those who embark on a Victory Lap. Here are nine of the best as far as we're concerned:

1. Victory Lap gives you the opportunity to start over and design a new life for yourself, but without being limited by your job or responsibilities to others. This time you're doing it for *you* not *them*, and you alone will decide your fate. It's no longer doing what you *have* to do; from now on it's all about what you *want* to do.

2. You turn your "paycheck" into a "playcheck." Because you have achieved some level of financial independence, you are working because you *want* to, not because you *have* to.

3. Moving on from being a good corporate soldier to leading a purposeful life, in which you're doing something you enjoy and that matters to you, may not pay as much in terms of money, but it pays a whole lot more in terms of spiritual meaning, personal health, and length and quality of life. In other words, some amount of meaningful work in your Victory Lap will keep you out of the graveyard longer.

4. You can opt to work part-time and free yourself up
   for eldercare, childcare, working out, charitable or
   philanthropic causes, travel, or any number of creative
   pursuits. You'll enjoy far more flexibility even though
   you're still working, and your schedule will be entirely
   under your control—not the Corp's.

5. Victory Lap Retirement gives you the opportunity to do
   the things you had to put off while you raised a family
   and accumulated wealth. It gives you the chance to
   pursue long-repressed dreams while you're still young
   enough to enjoy them and to create a long, successful,
   and sustainable lifestyle.

6. In Victory Lap Retirement, the goal is to achieve a
   simpler, more balanced lifestyle. Your Victory Lap
   allows you to become free-spirited, like a kid, again—a
   time when it seemed everything was possible.

7. In Victory Lap, you look for work that combines
   personal meaning and social purpose. The alignment
   of "who you are" with "what you do" is a powerful
   combination that will help maximize both passion and
   happiness. Helping others is the easiest way to get a
   happiness boost. Some may choose to work for pay,
   while others may choose to volunteer. In the end it's
   all about engaging in some form of work that creates
   purpose, gets the creative juices flowing, and gives you
   a reason to get out of bed each morning. Victory Lap
   Retirement will make you happy because you are doing
   work that you *want* to do and *on your own terms*. The
   work you choose will energize rather than deplete you
   because it's work that doesn't feel like work.

8. Victory Lap Retirement is the third act in a four-part play. It's a real shot at creating a truly balanced life, an opportunity to pursue lost dreams and missed opportunities. It gives you the chance to have many extra decades to do good work, enjoy yourself, spend more time with your spouse or partner, and relate in a more meaningful way to your family. It's an incredible chance to have fun, pursue old or new hobbies, make new friends, and possibly start checking off the boxes of your own unique "bucket list."

9. Victory Lap is not about who or what you used to be; it's all about who and what you will become. You should look at it as a rebirth, a "do over," a last shot at doing it right. Don't waste a great opportunity to "finally do it your way."

FINDING YOUR *IKIGAI*

The challenge is that after having most of your life structured for you while you were working, following orders, and doing what you were told, you now need to figure out what you want and how to create a lifestyle that will satisfy you for the rest of your life. That sort of freedom can be daunting for some people. On the positive side, by the time you reach Victory Lap, you will have the benefit of about fifty to sixty years of knowledge, skills, wisdom, insights, and experiences. At this point in your life, you know what you can do and can't do. You know what makes you happy and what doesn't. You know what matters to you and what doesn't. Use this knowledge to create your own version of a successful Victory Lap lifestyle.

Step one is to find work that you love, work that supports how you would really like to live. It should be based on something you enjoy doing, something you are good at, and something for which there is a need. And, ideally, something for which you can be paid! Once you find it, just do it. What are you waiting for?

It's important to understand we're all unique in what we need to be happy; everyone will have their own vision of *ikigai*. Please understand that one person's version is not better than another's. Some might choose to create a Victory Lap that satisfies their basic needs for social interaction and also gives them some extra income. Others, the so-called workaholics, may want their work to play a much larger part in their lives. This may seem to run counter to our goal for a stress-reduced lifestyle, but when you think about it, is it really stressful work if you are doing interesting work that you really enjoy doing? What's wrong with a strong work ethic? What's wrong with completely immersing yourself in a job you love doing?

A LESSON FROM MIKE'S FATHER

I remember when my father decided to retire. He was in charge of a large accounting department that went through a difficult enterprise-wide computer systems conversion late in his career. The constant high stress over a couple of years finally convinced him he had to leave to protect his health. However, being my father, he felt he had an obligation to the company to stay on until the project was completed, even though he suffered from high blood pressure. Staying there too long would have killed him, but as we later learned, leaving to do nothing wouldn't do him any good either. Death by stress or death by boredom—either way you cut it you end up dead!

Finally, he was able to retire when he turned sixty, but almost immediately he began to suffer from sudden retirement syndrome. The shock of leaving a long-term, successful career to do nothing created significant stress for him. He was unprepared for a full-stop retirement, and the drifting and boredom were causing him to lose it. Luckily my mother, who is a very smart woman, threw a copy of the want ads at him with a few opportunities circled. She said, "Here, stop whining and go find something to do." (My mother's Irish, can you tell?) It didn't take long before my father had a new part-time job delivering pet food to people at their homes.

When I first heard what he was doing, I had to laugh. Here was a former corporate executive who at one time had managed a group of about sixty people and now he was having the time of his life delivering pet food. But he didn't stop there. He was concerned about his health, so he decided to start cutting lawns as a side gig to get him into shape and also generate a little bit more fun money. My father had always been frugal and would never pay money to go to a gym, so instead he created his own workout program by cutting lawns, and, boy, was he ever happy with his new lifestyle. Minimal stress, no more deadlines, and he didn't have to manage people anymore.

You see, it doesn't have to be much, it doesn't have to be complicated. It's all up to you and what *you* need to do in order to be happy. That pet food job gave my father purpose and it made him feel good, especially delivering to older people who physically couldn't make it into the store. When they tried to tip him he wouldn't take it because the job for him wasn't about making money, it was about making him feel good, about feeling that he still mattered and that he could still contribute.

Some people view this time of their life as the last chance to chase their dreams; some just want a part-time job to help satisfy their social needs and generate a little extra income. Everyone has different needs and each one of us just has to find the right balance for ourselves, some combination of work and play that will make us happy. And many people have discovered that it doesn't take much at all.

So what can you take away from the story about Mike's father so that you can optimize your own version of Victory Lap?

1. It's important to change the way you view the connection between money and self-worth. Some people think, "I can't do that job, it's below me and will not pay me what I'm worth." In Victory Lap you no longer use money as a measurement, as a way of comparing yourself with others; you simply use it to help finance the things you want to do with your increased leisure time, like going on fun adventures with your family. Remember, it's your *play*check, not your paycheck now.

2. Knowing that you are counted on, that you are valued, gives you a good reason to get up in the morning and will add years to your life. Studies have clearly shown that the sudden loss of a person's traditional role can have a measurable effect on mortality. You die quickly if you feel like you are invisible and are no longer needed. Work—any kind of work—gives you a feeling of responsibility, of making a contribution, of mattering.

3. To ensure a high quality Victory Lap, it's important to socialize and have the benefit of a social network. Work gives you the chance to surround yourself with fun, interesting people.

A LESSON FROM ROB'S FATHER

I can think of no better example of a successful Victory Lapper than my dad. It turns out he was a bit of a pioneer in the Victory Lap space, leaving the corporate world in 1991 at the age of fifty. I can happily report that he finally fully retired at the end of 2017, nearly thirty years later! His Victory Lap story starts like many others I've known, with corporate consolidation and upheaval.

My father was in the airline industry for nearly all of his career, starting in the late 1950s. While the '60s and '70s were a time of great expansion and growth for the still-burgeoning industry, deregulation in 1978 started a massive consolidation of commercial carriers and a multi-decade fare war. My father saw his original employer, Ozark Air Lines, acquired by TWA in 1986, which brought a major regime and cultural change. After several years in this new environment, my dad decided enough was enough. He resigned and started his own consulting business.

It was a nervous transition at first. The turning point for him, as he's told me on several occasions, was getting an "anchor client." Within a few months of leaving TWA, he had been engaged to do some lobbying work for a group that would provide enough revenue for him to support our family's core expenses. Once he had this covered, he added clients and grew his income until he had virtually replaced his prior income as an airline executive.

You could argue that this wasn't really the beginning of his Victory Lap. After all, he was barely fifty years old and for the first ten years after leaving the airline he worked pretty hard. As a lobbyist, he traveled a lot, still working full-time and putting in consistently long hours. He was really building a new business for himself, ultimately using it to take a successful Victory Lap. The last ten to fifteen years of his consulting practice were particularly important to that end. As my father entered his sixties, he had a number of clients and all the business he could handle. At a certain point he stopped saying yes to new opportunities unless they really interested him. He also began to increase his price and terms of work. From a lifestyle perspective, he was able to make work and life look seamless at this stage. He worked hard at times, when needed, but he played plenty of golf, traveled, and was able to attend every grandchild's major milestone events (academic, religious, or athletic).

Year after year, Dad and I would have a discussion about his work. As we reviewed my parents' annually updated financial plan, he would often ask me, "Do you think I should stop working?"

"Not if you still enjoy what you're doing," I would usually respond.

His lower consulting income was enough, combined with some pension income, so that he and my mom were able to delay Social Security and portfolio withdrawals completely until they were well into their seventies. He got an extra decade of growth on his investments as a result, which now makes the next couple of decades much easier for us to plan.

Dad elected to take what I call the "Glidepath" approach to his eventual retirement (another way to express the Victory Lap idea), working slightly less every year until he was down to just one client for the last two to three years of his business. While he worked full-time initially, he probably averaged thirty hours a week during the core years, and much less over the last five to ten years. Near the end of his working life, it seemed as if he was completely retired except for staying caught up on industry news, participating in conference calls, and being available for a consult when needed. In many ways that minimal engagement is the pinnacle of a consultant's pricing power, "We'll pay you to take our call."

THE IT'S-TOO-LATE TRAP

An all-too-common phenomenon is what we call the "it's too late" trap. It doesn't seem to matter what age you are and what life dream you've been postponing, an oft-used rationalization tends to be something like, "Well, if I had only started activity X back when I was twenty, things would be different. But now that I'm [plug in your current age here], it's just too late to make a change."

Now it's true that certain professions are best entered while you have a young and healthy body. We don't know too many athletes who decide to become NHL hockey players after the age of thirty-five or forty, for example. But if you're a modern office-dwelling "knowledge worker" or "symbol manipulator," odds are you're mostly using your mind, not your body. If anything, the mind just gets stronger with use over the years and your cranium gets filled with all sorts of knowledge a younger person may not possess.

The subtitle to Joyce Meyer's book *You Can Begin Again* is also the book's key message: *No Matter What, It's Never Too Late.* Meyer discovered that this theme runs throughout the Bible, although it certainly also applies to daily life. It turns out that doors may close for a reason, but as the old saying goes, when one does shut, you can be sure another is sure to open soon after. You may think you've come up with a plan, call it Plan A, but Meyer points out that unbeknownst to you, the Almighty may already have put into motion Plan B. And the B stands for "Better!" In this way, failure (or perceived failure, like being fired, a business failing, or a divorce) can clear the way and set you up for future success.

The point is that it's never too late to launch a second act and rev your engines for a satisfying Victory Lap or encore career. Try to rid yourself of the notion that fifty years old (or sixty, seventy, or any other age) is "too old" or "too late" to start something new.

Odds are that if you take care of yourself, eat properly, exercise regularly, avoid smoking and other life-shortening habits, you'll have an excellent chance of reaching age 100. If so, then fifty is just the half-way mark! You'd have fifty more years to retrain and launch your encore career, and even to master that new calling and become one of the world's leading practitioners of it.

ROB ON A VICTORY LAP PIONEER

I recently listened to a podcast episode of NPR's *How I Built This* and heard the fascinating story of Bob and Charlee Moore, the founders of Bob's Red Mill, makers of an array of natural foods that you've probably seen in your grocery store. Having started Bob's Red Mill in 1978, Bob Moore may be one of the pioneers in the natural/organic food space, but he's also a pioneer of Victory Lap Retirement. Bob is eighty-nine years old and he started his company in 1978, after he retired and went back to school! His love for milling whole grains and helping people fueled him to build a terrific cereal and grain business and he continues working every day. He sees no need to ever retire because he loves what he's doing and is purpose driven. I highly recommend the episode and the Bob's Red Mill website if you'd like to be inspired by Bob and Charlee Moore's story.

The encore-career literature is full of examples of supposedly "old" people who launched the career that gained them world fame only after they had reached the age of traditional retirement. Think of Anna Mary Robertson "Grandma" Moses, who began painting in earnest at seventy-eight; or fast food kings Ray Kroc and Colonel Harland Sanders, both of whom launched their firms (McDonald's and Kentucky Fried Chicken respectively) after their fiftieth birthdays. There are many more similar examples. So if you catch yourself saying, "It's too late to start anything new," do what mothers used to do to their children who let loose swear words. Wash your mouth out with soap!

Come to view the phrase "it's too late" as nothing more than what it actually is: an excuse for staying in your rut and refusing to face your fears and conquer them. It's just another dream-killer. So whatever it is you dream of doing—be it learning a musical instrument; writing a novel or a screenplay; or becoming a rock star or a painter or an actor or an ordained minister or an in-demand platform speaker or any of a thousand other possible encore careers—just grit your teeth and start doing it.

HAVE, DO, BE

Remember this simple formula: Have, do, be. The first step is obtaining the tool or instrument required to practice your new craft. It may be a piano, a guitar, a palette and paints, or a computer equipped with a word processor. Having acquired the tool, you need to use it: do the painting, do the writing, play the musical instrument. And after a period of doing it, you will one day realize that you have become this new person: you *are* a painter, writer, or musician, and an entire new career is launched—perhaps one that will not only be satisfying, but one that may also carry the bonus of paying you for practicing it. Recall the song from the cult film, *The Rocky Horror Picture Show*, and the classic lyric, "Don't dream it. Be it." Too late to dream it? Balderdash! Have, do, be.

4

Create a Life from Which You Don't Have to Retire

The biggest adventure you can ever take is to live the life of your dreams.

—Oprah Winfrey

No one could accuse Oprah Winfrey of failing to think big and live the life of her dreams. Despite the odds against her when she started out, Oprah became a one-woman media empire. She is over sixty and, even though her net worth is in the billions, she shows little sign of wishing to retire because she loves what she does. Why would any of us want to retire if we found something that we can be passionate about, even if we have somewhat less wealth than the famous Ms. Winfrey? The challenge is to find out what your innermost dreams are, then create a life from which you may never want to retire, as long as you are physically and mentally able to keep up the pace (even if a slightly more leisurely pace than your primary career).

Work while you play, play while you work.

The most common term used to describe late-life career changes is an encore career, often termed an encore act or second act. There are many great resources for boomers interested in finding or creating an encore career. You could start by typing either of those terms on Amazon. One book you'll find that we highly recommend, is Marc Freedman's *Encore: Finding Work that Matters in the Second Half of Life*. Also check out the companion website that Freedman founded at Encore.org and, for a Canadian perspective, take a look www.challengefactory.ca.

Once you have done the homework and identified what route you want to take in your Victory Lap, you'll need to create a plan based on prudent, well-researched moves prior to jumping into it.

YOUR VICTORY LAP IS LIMITED ONLY BY YOUR IMAGINATION

There isn't enough space here to do justice to the various options available in a typical Victory Lap trajectory, and new ones are being created all the time. Scenarios range from the story of Professor Fred Kummerow and the people employed at Vita Needle (see chapter 1) to the lifestyle created by Mike's father, who got joy and satisfaction out of delivering pet food and other odd jobs. The point is that the lifestyle you create is unique to you: all that matters is that it's meaningful and that it works for you and only you.

While there are a number of approaches you could take to finance your Victory Lap, in Rob's advisory practice they have noticed two primary financial strategies emerge, which we refer to as the Glidepath and Passion/Hobby strategy. It's important to understand these two main options to design the Victory Lap that's right for you.

Glidepath Strategy

This strategy is most common among those whose primary objective in a Victory Lap is to work on their own terms. They like what they do, they would just like to do less of it and, depending upon the type of work they do, they may continue working well into their seventies, eighties, or later. Working less reduces the stress in their lives and frees up time for the other things that are important to them: friends and family, eldercare, working out, leisure activities, and traveling, for example. Rob has seen numerous professionals (doctors, lawyers, accountants, etc.) Glidepath their way into retirement over a very long period with relative ease.

In a Glidepath approach, the individual looks to continue applying the skills, relationships, and experience they have in a new, more manageable packaging. There are several different ways to implement this strategy.

The simplest way to Glidepath into retirement is to continue working with your current employer, or with another organization in the same industry, but on a part-time basis. With 10,000 baby boomers leaving the workforce every day, corporations are increasingly open to older experienced employees transitioning to part-time work. If your current employer doesn't allow for it, maybe a competitor will.

The classic example of Glidepathing is a businessperson or professional who transitions from being an employee to becoming a consultant. You become your own boss and sometimes your first and largest client is your previous employer (as was the case for Rob's dad in chapter 3). Companies increasingly support this approach to retain the experience of a long-time, valued employee who would be hard (and costly) to replace. The benefit to the employee is that consulting allows them to extend their income-earning years while gaining a significant measure of control and flexibility over their schedule and workload, which translates into a lot less stress.

Another example of a Glidepath strategy is coaching and/or teaching. Remember Rob's good friend from chapter 2 who was formerly a global marketing executive and is now doing both consulting and teaching? He is having a blast, working hard at times and completely "off the grid" at others. He recently said that although his income is only a fraction of what it once was, the work he now does feels more like play. When the line between work and play becomes blurry, you know you are on the right track.

Rob's friend isn't working directly with his former company, but he is applying all of the considerable experience, skills, and wisdom he developed over his career there in the work he now does with numerous clients in several industries. The moral of this story is that it's hard to lose when you can make some money doing something that you are good at and love doing.

Be aware that a Glidepath strategy typically involves a reduction in income and benefits, including health insurance, disability, and life insurance benefits, so it's important to understand how these cutbacks may impact your overall financial plan. We'll discuss this further in chapter 6.

Passion/Hobby Strategy

While Glidepathing is the most common and lowest-risk strategy of the two main Victory Lap options, we're truly inspired when someone decides to venture outside their comfort zone and take a swing for the fences.

- A data analytics professional who begins making custom furniture, a teacher who becomes a fishing charter captain, or a former CFO who decides to open a retail wine shop.
- Maybe you want to go back to school or start that small business you have always been dreaming about.
- Maybe you want to volunteer and help drill water wells in Africa like Mike's friend Wayne.
- Maybe you want to become a gourmet cook, or a stand-up comedian, or a writer, web site designer, teacher.

These are all examples of people who have left, or might consider leaving, their primary career completely behind to pursue "bucket list" types of jobs that more directly satisfy their hobbies, personal interests, and passions. Shifting lanes this dramatically may require some additional education, licensing, and other preparation. But it's well worth the effort if you truly love the work and it provides enough income to make it worth the time and money spent to make it happen, or if you are in a financial position to afford making the investment in some training or starting such a business without the need for any significant income. The possibilities are endless and the only one holding you back from doing these things is you.

Here are a few more interesting examples of Victory Lap careers fueled by personal passions and hobbies. Some involve a degree of seasonality and could really be thought of as forms of mini-retirement.

- After leaving his corporate job, Don—a self-professed golf nut—found employment at a high-end golf club during the summer. In addition to hanging out with golfers and talking about golf all day, one of the perks for Don is that he can golf for free. He and his wife spend their winters in Mexico, where he spends most of his time playing, you guessed it, golf.

- Frank, on the other hand, just loves to fish. Soon after retirement he bought a small fishing lodge up north. In a good year he barely breaks even, but he just loves fishing and hanging out with other fishermen. He spends his winters in Belize, where his wife relaxes while he fly fishes for bonefish.

- Harry and his wife owned their own clothing business but sold it when Harry turned sixty-seven. His wife was the first to go back to work, working part-time at a store that specialized in wedding dresses. Harry followed soon after once he completed the sale of their large home and the process of downsizing to a condo. He just celebrated his twentieth year working in a store specializing in suits for kids, where he just loves interacting with the parents.

- John is an artist who's pretty handy with tools. He's built a business building and selling sheds and Muskoka chairs while at his cottage in the summer.

- Ron, who was always good with a guitar, went on vacation one year to St. Martin and decided to stay. He started playing at a restaurant on the boardwalk to help attract new customers from all the passengers coming off the many cruise ships that visit each winter. Ron, one might say, has the life of Riley!

• Jim and Ellen left successful careers in marketing and advertising and are now serving as explorers, scouting areas in Southeast Asia where boomers can enjoy an affordable retirement. They have their own blog, www.planet-boomer.com, and have also written a book about their adventures called *Planet Boomer: Retire Now for Less in Southeast Asia.*

WHAT FORM WILL YOUR VICTORY LAP TAKE?

If you're still in your primary career it's a good idea to start planning your Victory Lap now, whether it will be driven by Glidepathing or by monetizing a passion or hobby. If leaving traditional employment behind (even a part-time job) and forging ahead on your own is appealing to you, there are a number of potential business models you should consider before taking the plunge. It's important to figure out which one fits your personality and your retirement goals. If you know you want to be your own boss, why not give yourself a head start and structure the Victory Lap that will work best for you?

Some may argue that they don't have time to plan all this out, but think about just how much time we all waste every day. The average American watches more than 1,600 hours of television each year, which is the equivalent of 200 eight-hour work days. If you applied the same amount of time to starting a part-time business, you would be far ahead of the average American. Imagine, through the power of compounding, what you could accomplish over a ten-year period. Stop thinking and just start.

ROB ON WINE-DING DOWN

One of our favorite clients was an executive with a home builder for most of his career and decided to pull his golden para-
chute in his early fifties. With a big enough nest egg to cover
the costs of college for their kids and be retired, he and his
wife moved out of state to a more rural setting. But a few years
into their retirement, they had an itch to scratch. They realized
they were too young for rocking chairs and wanted to start
their own business.

As avid wine drinkers and collectors, they saw a need in their
local community for a specialty wine shop. They had moved to
an area that had grown into a popular summer tourist spot. Like
many small towns–turned tourism centers, it lacked specialty retail outlets like wine shops. Our clients filled the bill and opened
their own wine business, which they ran for a number of years.

While they didn't get into it for the money, it was a great
little business for their community and it allowed them to do
something they enjoyed while spending their time together as
empty nesters! Even though they sold the wine store after a
few years, it was a fun and fulfilling chapter on their road to full
retirement.

Starting Your Own Business

All our dreams can come true if we have the courage to pursue them.
—Walt Disney

A dream is your creative vision for your life in the future.
You must break out of your current comfort zone and become
comfortable with the unfamiliar and the unknown.
—Denis Waitley

If you accept the thesis that, in general, people will continue to live longer than was once anticipated, it hardly seems unreasonable for financially independent baby boomers who have left giant corporations to embrace a brand new work life. As we make clear in this book at several junctures, if you believe your health is robust enough to put you in the extended life expectancy camp, it's definitely not too late to try something new if you've only just reached your fifties or sixties. Try thinking of yourself as being merely at the halfway mark of life, with decades of healthy living—and working—ahead of you.

Our term for late-bloomer baby boomer entrepreneurs is "Boomerpreneur." Boomerpreneurs are free to follow their dreams. They are like starving artists who care more about their art than the pursuit of material wealth, except they aren't starving, because they have achieved financial independence. Knowing that your basic needs are met—whether it be the funds for food, utilities, property taxes, and the like—frees you up to take on longer-term projects: projects like writing a book or creating a website like the Financial Independence Hub (to cite just two examples near and dear to our hearts!).

Boomerpreneurs are builders who try to create something, perhaps something they dreamed about for most of their lives but never had the chance to attempt. Dreams are powerful: they energize your mind, ignite your passion, and drive you to do everything you can in order to achieve them. Chasing after a dream and finally catching it is one of the happiest and most fulfilling things you could ever do.

In Victory Lap, Boomerpreneurs know exactly where they want to go, what is important to them, what they want, and what will make them happy. They gain strength from knowing that after so many years they are finally in control of their own destiny. Now *they're* the ones who make the big decisions.

MIKE ON TAKING THE LEAP

Going to work for someone else on a part-time basis is far easier than starting your own business from scratch. But for some of us, especially the ones who need a high degree of autonomy in order to be happy, like me, being your own boss and not having to take orders from someone else is well worth the pain.

Starting your own business is probably the hardest thing you'll ever do. Your resolve will be tested and out of necessity you will be forced to learn a lot of new things. You'll be working harder than you ever have, making decisions on the fly, and operating way outside your comfort zone.

When attempting to start my own business I kept asking myself the same question over and over again: Was it worth all the effort, headaches, and stress? And the answer always ended up being, yes.

Having an opportunity to help people your way is well worth the price of admission because it opens up a whole new world to you, one that you've never experienced before. For the first time you have the freedom to call the shots, and believe me, freedom is a beautiful thing!

Following are some of the top advantages that come with being self-employed, no matter what kind of business you're in or what motivates you.

1. Satisfaction derived from being in control of your work and being your own boss. It's your business, done your way.

2. Ability to create your own work-life balance. A key benefit is the flexibility this lifestyle allows. You're able to set your own hours, so you can work hard when

you want to, take time off when you feel like it, and sometimes even work in your pajamas if you want to.

3. You constantly challenge yourself. You compete, learn new things and, as a result, grow.
4. You increase the size of your social circle by connecting with your clients and suppliers.
5. You can choose who you want to work with and surround yourself with positive people who care about you.
6. Building your own business, helping others, and being successful gives a big boost to you in terms of personal satisfaction. When you help others you really are helping yourself.

Partnering Up

If you ask Mike, he'll be the first to admit that he sucks at technology, but he is good at public speaking, writing, and coaching. One of the smartest things he did when he went out on his own was to team up with Gerry, who can speak computer and handles all the tech stuff that Mike is neither good at nor has an interest in learning, but needs desperately to help his business run efficiently. Mike and Gerry each have different skills that they bring to the table; teaming up allows Mike to play to his strengths and that makes him happy. Because of Gerry he has less stress and more fun, and that is what a Victory Lap Retirement is all about.

If you're thinking about going into business for yourself in your own Victory Lap, why would you waste valuable time trying to learn something that you will never master or like doing, when you could avoid all that pain and just partner up with someone who knows what they are doing?

Partnering up can be an informal arrangement like Mike has with Gerry, in which you connect with other professionals with complementary skills to help one another. Or it can be a more

formal working relationship: perhaps actually going into business with someone else to spread the risk, share a built-in support
network, tap into each other's contacts to grow more business,
or simply to enjoy fulfilling work with a like-minded partner,
friend, or colleague.

ROB ON PARTNERSHIP

I recently met with an attorney that my firm often recommends
to clients for estate planning and corporate and transactional
work. About five years ago, he left a large suburban law firm
in our area to start his own firm in his mid-fifties. Bill had spent
all of his career working for others but decided he was ready
to partner up with another experienced and well respected
attorney in the area to start a firm of their own. He and I have
talked about Victory Lap Retirement many times in the past. In
our last conversation, he said he realized that starting his own
law firm is his Victory Lap!

With their firm established, he now has exponentially more
control and enjoyment in serving clients on a platform that he
created with the core values of excellence, transparency, and in-
tegrity. He is having a ball doing it and isn't in any hurry to stop.
He still has some runway and wants to continue working close
to full-time for the foreseeable future.

While on the surface it might appear that Bill isn't really on
a Victory Lap at all, he would strongly disagree. He is no longer
beholden to the requirements and structure of a firm that does
not share his values and vision, has greater work-life balance,
and generally greater enjoyment of his work and the flexibility
that comes with owning your own business. Why would Bill retire from something that he loves doing?

Of course spreading the risk with a partner also means sharing the rewards. You might be reluctant to give up a part of your new business (it's human nature), but just remember that 100 percent of nothing is nothing, but 50 percent of something is something. Why go it alone when there is a better, easier way by partnering up with someone?

ROB'S CLIENT: FROM CORPORATE GUN TO BUSINESS OWNER

Andy is a favorite client of our firm. He's a terrific family steward and former COO at a sporting goods company. After his employer's downsizing, Andy took the better part of a year to evaluate his options.

While opportunities would no doubt come for other corporate roles, Andy decided he wanted to blaze his own path in his mid-fifties. He engaged in an expansive research and networking process to learn about opportunities to buy a local business. After nearly a year, he found a terrific landscaping design and construction business in the area and bought it. He partnered with the founder and transitioned the business over a period of months.

Every time we talk, Andy is enthused with his company. He loves the work he's doing, imparting his knowledge and experience directly into a business he owns! The experience and rewards have been tremendous and we can't wait to see how Andy parlays it into more enjoyment and success over the next few years!

Buying an Existing Business

In Rob's financial planning practice, one of the more common Victory Lap scenarios they see is for a client to leave their job as a corporate executive and buy a small business. For someone who has operated in the often politically-charged culture of a massive organization, acquiring a solid small business and working as an owner-operator can be an exciting last chapter of work.

The opportunity to take on a small company, buy out a founder who's ready to transition out, and be an owner-operator seems exhilarating to an increasing number of successful clients we know. Good income potential, more control and flexibility, and an asset that has the potential to grow in value, have been enough to entice a few folks we know to ditch the corporate herd for their own path.

TRANSITIONS CAN TAKE LONGER THAN YOU THINK

There's a good chance your original plan or business model will not be the one you finally end up with; plans evolve, so be open to tweaking things. Always listen to and go with your inner voice. If it's telling you that you need to change things, then go ahead and make the required changes. At some point your inner voice will whisper that you are attracted to something. You feel excitement, a sense of alignment, happiness, clarity, a knowing that this is the thing, the right thing for you to do. Don't be afraid. Just do it!

This change of direction is exactly what happened to Mike after he joined his wife's wealth management business. At first he had planned on becoming an investment adviser focusing on succession planning for family-owned businesses. But as he talked to more and more people, he felt the need to help others with their fear of retirement and assist them with their transition into their own version of a Victory Lap. Having never written before, he never would have considered writing blogs, nor for that matter helping to write the book you are currently holding. Funny how plans change!

SHOULD YOU ANNOUNCE YOUR PLANS FOR A VICTORY LAP?

Of course you're incredibly excited when you hit upon that purpose to which you want to dedicate the next phase of your life, when you're juiced by the prospect of a new part-time career, or when you can't wait to be in control of your own schedule and your own destiny in your Victory Lap. Naturally you want to share your exciting plans with everyone around you, including your colleagues in the Corp you're leaving, and maybe even your boss. But be careful, bosses can start to act a little strangely after you tell them you plan to leave the company at some point in the future.

It's an unfair assumption, but upon hearing of your future intentions your boss may believe you are no longer fully committed to your job and that your performance will start to slide as you focus on getting ready for your new career. This can cause some friction, so it's best to make sure you have the bulk of your Victory Lap preparation completed prior to dropping the bomb, just in case.

In Mike's case, within three months of having declared he was planning to leave the Corp, he was pleasantly surprised to receive a buyout from the company. Was it a coincidence? Who knows, but it's better to receive a payout than a gold watch any day. The bonus is that Mike's lump-sum payment generated some liquidity until his new business started to generate a profit.

TWO CASH FLOW OPTIONS

Before you take the leap to start living the Victory Lap you've envisioned for yourself, it's important to understand, as we've said before, that out of the gate your Victory Lap could result in a sizeable pay cut until your business gains traction. Before you start leading the Victory Lap lifestyle, it would be wise to focus on paying off your big expenses: wait until the kids are out of college, the mortgage is paid off, and you are out of debt. Also consider the possibility of downsizing. Or plan to rely on your partner's income as a safety net so you can sleep at night. And always have a back-up plan in case things don't work out.

Part of getting your financial house in order is figuring out how you will replace your employment income to cover your lifestyle expenses during a Victory Lap chapter in your life. Depending on your specific situation, there are myriad ways you could consider doing this. We'll get into more detail in chapter 6 on how to figure out how much you'll need in retirement and how to create a spending plan; for now, we'll oversimplify it here with two broad approaches to ensuring that you have sufficient, sustainable cash flow:

1. Passive Income + Playcheck
2. Work to Live

Neither is superior and there are trade-offs to both. Which route you choose really depends on your unique variables and situation, so you'll want to consider carefully and match your strategy to the strengths and priorities of your own plan.

Passive Income + Playcheck

This approach is quite simple and is used by people who have already achieved a comfortable level of financial independence by the time they are leaving the corporate world behind, whether by choice or they've been pushed out. For our purposes, this is the point where your "fixed" expenses (non-discretionary) are covered by your passive (non-work) income. Examples of passive income sources include:

- Dividend and interest income from your investments
- Company pensions and government pensions (Social Security, or Canada Pension Plan and Old Age Security)
- Rental income from real estate investments
- Royalties from intellectual properties, such as books, music, apps

In this scenario, you no longer need to work to cover your core expenses: to keep a roof over your head, put food on the table, and pay for the basic necessities (heating, electricity, property taxes, income taxes, etc.). They will be paid for by the annual cash flow from your passive income.

Let's take a simple example. Say your annual core, fixed expenses are $30,000. That means that in your Victory Lap, you would have to generate $30,000 in annual after-tax passive (non-work) income to be financially independent.

Beyond that, any extra money you earn during your Victory Lap (part-time work, business income, etc.) would cover your discretionary spending, allowing you to live beyond a survival lifestyle. This is the money you spend on entertainment, vacations and travel, hobbies, eating out, club memberships, and other luxuries that fill your life with color, richness, and fun.

Someone who has enough passive income to pay their fixed expenses could now choose to work exclusively to cover their discretionary expenses. Keep in mind, these items do add up and could require a decent level of income, especially if you have expensive hobbies like a country club, boat, or travel abroad. That said, having the flexibility to work less and create balance can be very exciting for a lot of potential Victory Lappers. Some may even be able to take on only seasonal, project, or contract work that will keep them busy at times and allow for significant travel or chunks of downtime in other periods of the year.

This approach works particularly well for people who have low fixed lifestyle costs. Often these people live simply, have no mortgage or rent, own cash-positive cash-flow assets (like rental property) or have accrued significant pension benefits from a long career in larger organizations. Victory Lappers taking this approach are also likely to be at least in their late fifties or early sixties—old enough that they qualify to draw on retirement accounts, company pensions, and/or Social Security or other government benefits.

Work to Live

Another option applies to individuals who, after doing the math, determine that they will be able to generate enough active income from the work they choose to do in their Victory Lap to cover all their monthly bills (fixed and discretionary). They can, therefore, defer drawing on their investments and pensions as long as they are still working in their Victory Lap and earning enough income, allowing these assets to continue growing in value, which results in greater long-term security.

For example, say an executive working for a Corp has a salary of $100,000 with an expected bonus of $20,000. That's $120,000 of total earned income prior to taxes. If we deduct estimated taxes of 25 percent, we are left with $90,000 of spendable income.

Let's also assume that this individual has been saving $20,000 per year into their 401k (the equivalent is a Registered Retirement Savings Plan, or RRSP, in Canada), and another $5,000 per year into a brokerage account. In addition, let's assume that the mortgage payment for their home is $1,500 a month ($18,000 per year, not including taxes and insurance) and that the balance is close to being paid off. If over the next couple of years, while preparing to take a Victory Lap, this executive can pay off the mortgage, then real annual outflows needed in Victory Lap are $47,000:

$90K	(CURRENT AFTER-TAX INCOME)
– $25K	(SAVINGS & INVESTMENTS)
– $18K	(MORTGAGE)
$47K	REAL SPENDING

This is the amount required to cover both their core, non-discretionary living expenses and their discretionary lifestyle costs. Generating active income of $47,000 after tax is now the new target for any work done in Victory Lap. This executive, who was presumably working hard to make $120,000 per year in employment income, can explore consulting, teaching, or project work with the aim of making less than half of what he or she made in a stressful job in the Corp. Easing up in this fashion in Victory Lap takes the pressure off and gives a person the time and flexibility to do the things they were unable to do when they were working full out. All the while, this individual's retirement savings can continue to grow while they defer any distributions until a later date.

MIKE ON THE POWER OF FINANCIAL FREEDOM

Both Jonathan and I are following the Passive Income + Playcheck approach in our own Victory Laps (Rob hasn't started his yet and is still working full-time). The only regret we both share is that we should have started this phase of our lives sooner.

In my case, after achieving financial independence I wasn't scared about losing my job anymore. I knew that the passive income that was being generated from my investments and other assets would cover all our fixed expenses. I could finally sleep at night knowing that no matter what happened, my family and I would be okay.

Although I found it hard to leave a high-income job late in my career, it was one of the best decisions I ever made. My financial independence gave me the courage to leave a job that bored me and it felt so good not having to manage others anymore, nor having to compete and trying to win all the time.

Achieving financial independence gave me my personal freedom back—the freedom to be me—and allowed me to regain control over how I spend my time. Now I get to do what I want to do when I want to, and I'm very grateful for that.

If I don't want to do something then I don't do it. The power of being able to say "no" is freedom in its purest sense, something that we all crave inside. It's such a beautiful feeling but it took me some time adjusting because I hadn't been free for a long time.

I have achieved a level of financial independence in which my basic living expenses are covered by the retirement assets that I have managed to accumulate over the years. My discretionary lifestyle expenses—the gym, vacation trips with the family, entertainment, and so on—are covered by my playcheck, the extra money I earn in my Victory Lap through my retirement coaching, books, and seminars. I've created work for myself that I enjoy, so to me it doesn't feel like work at all. And even better, I can keep doing it for as long as I like.

Like most of you, I've spent most of my life worrying about money. Thankfully, I don't waste time doing that anymore. My financial adviser is so good I ended up marrying her (inside joke)! I've had a lifelong interest in investing and always managed my own portfolio. When I left my banking job, I rolled over my pension (taking the lump-sum value and investing it in an individual retirement account). Managing that money and the investment mix myself not only gives me complete control over it, but also allows me to ensure that any of my retirement assets that remain after I die will serve as a legacy for the Contessa (my wife) and the kids.

Currently I have a retirement portfolio that is fully invested in blue-chip, dividend paying stocks. My wife's job is to monitor the companies that I own stock in to ensure the safety of the dividend and to look for other attractive blue-chip buying opportunities. This frees me from watching the market daily, on BNN (our equivalent in Canada to CNBC) or my iPhone. I intend on staying fully invested for the long term, so I don't lose any sleep over market fluctuations or corrections. My only priority is that the dividends keep rolling in. A dividend increase feels like Christmas came early!

This is what works for me and allows me to sleep well at night. Everyone's situation is different, so it is important to craft a lifestyle and financial plan that works for you. If you are unsure of your financial situation, talking to a qualified financial adviser or financial planner is highly recommended. This is *not* an area you want to leave to chance.

KEY CONSIDERATIONS FOR YOUR VICTORY LAP

Victory Laps don't just happen; you need to *make* yours happen. Have specific plans and goals in place that are in harmony with what you want out of this phase of your life. Following are some important things to consider when planning your Victory Lap.

1. The best time to plan for Victory Lap Retirement is a few years prior to making the jump. You want to be well prepared and have your financial house in order before making the move.

2. Find a job or create one that matches up with the skills and talents that are your strengths. Play to your strengths whenever possible.

3. Identify any additional education, skills, and training required prior to starting your Victory Lap, then work on adding them to your Victory Lap Retirement arsenal.

4. Find work you are passionate about, something you are proud of and that is important to you. It should be work you find challenging and interesting, that awakens your creativity and may even provide a decent level of income. Avoid doing something you do not enjoy. Seek work that lets you see the personal contribution you are making and the results that flow from that contribution.

5. Identify mentors and reach out to your network of social and professional contacts for help and guidance. Surround yourself with positive, supportive people. Create a support team that will cheer you on and help

you get there. Talk to those who have already gone there and done it. Often other people can see a solution that you can't because they are not as emotionally invested in the situation; you're just too close to your own situation to judge. This is where a good money coach, financial adviser, or even a life coach may be of great benefit. Don't be too proud to ask for help if you need it.

6. Find a role model and copy what he or she did. If that person did it, why can't you?

7. You need to do your homework and come up with an idea, then research options about how to make it happen before you pull the trigger. Have someone review your plan and test it for soundness. Take a calculated risk rather than throwing caution to the wind. At this time in your life, you don't have as long to recover from a financial setback, so do your best to minimize the risk and maximize your chances of success going into your Victory Lap.

8. If possible, take some time off before starting your Victory Lap. You need to be mentally ready to make the change. Take a breather of perhaps three months so you can regroup, recharge, and collect yourself. This is like taking a racehorse and putting it on the farm for a "freshening period" after a long, hard campaign. Tired horses don't run well, and neither will you. In these days of corporate restructuring, the severance package that often accompanies layoffs can give both precious time and money to contemplate your next move. By all

means, at least take a week or two vacation first, then enter research-and-networking mode.

9. To start your Victory Lap, you need to get physically fit and create an energetic appearance and mindset. When you are fit you feel good, and people pick up on the positive vibes you are sending out. We all like people with a positive attitude, and we're drawn to them.

10. Last but certainly not least, make sure your spouse or partner is on board!

Victory Lap lets you re-imagine your life and allows for renewal and adventure. This time in your life is about *your* choice, *your* rules, *your* way. This is your chance to create a meaningful life of challenge and purpose for yourself. It won't always be easy—the best things in life never are—but with effort comes a sense of accomplishment, which makes the victory in the end so much sweeter.

5

The Economics of a Victory Lap

The Longevity Play

It is not realistic to finance a 30-year retirement with 30 years of work. You can't expect to put 10% of your income aside and then finance a retirement that's just as long.
—John Shoven, Stanford University professor of economics

While the allure of leaving the corporate jungle behind and taking a Victory Lap is compelling for most of us, the financial concerns alone are enough to thwart many would-be Victory Lap candidates. As a financial planner, Rob can't count how many times he has seen a client begin to consider "changing lanes" in his or her career, only to hesitate due to the financial uncertainty surrounding such a move. They often feel as if they have financial "handcuffs" with their current job that are too good to leave, particularly when the alternative is unclear to them.

It's too easy for most of us simply to continue down the current path, to stay with our job, keep saving, and hope for the best. The reality is, it's actually risky staying put and doing nothing. Corporate employees found that out the hard way during the Great Recession (2008-09) as companies laid off workers at all levels. Job security didn't exist, particularly for older employees.

The field of behavioral finance would label employee loyalty as a *familiarity bias*. It's a bias that adversely affects our decision making, often compelling us to under-appreciate the risks involved in sticking with our current situation because we are familiar with the company, job, or industry. It's always easier for an outsider to see the risk because the outsider doesn't have the same familiarity bias as the individual in the situation. The bottom line is that we bear risk every day with our current employer, whether we realize it or not.

Admittedly, there are also risks to leaving your employer, but there are some important and compelling *advantages* to a successful Victory Lap that are worth detailing. In our experience, the Victory Lap version of retirement is often more financially sound than sticking around the corporate jungle for as long as you can. This may sound counterintuitive, but it's true. The main reason? Longevity of income. Financially speaking, longevity of income, *any income*, is a significant variable when considering retirement and is perhaps the most important argument for Victory Lap Retirement as an improvement over the traditional work-retirement model.

In other words, when you design a Victory Lap for yourself in which you work because you want to, not because you have to, you are likely to keep doing what you love to some extent well into the future, beyond when you would normally have retired. The income you continue to earn in your Victory Lap—whether that's a little fun money to cover discretionary expenses, or more substantial funds to cover all your living costs—will go a long way to financing a sustainable retirement lifestyle and ensuring that your money will last as long as you do.

THE BETTER WAY TO FUND YOUR RETIREMENT

As we described in chapter 1, retirement periods on average are getting much longer than they were 75 to 100 years ago. As planners, we regularly create models for clients based on a two-person, thirty-year retirement that assumes one or both spouses living to at least age ninety. With the rapid decline of corporate pensions, and government benefits only covering a portion of the average retiree's spending in retirement, there are really only two viable choices to fund the bulk of your retirement:

1. Save enough by day one of retirement to replace upwards of 70-80 percent of your current income (the portion not covered by pensions, etc.) or;

2. Gradually begin your retirement while continuing to generate some level of active (work) income.

We refer to option 1 as "The Nest Egg," that is, the conventional full-stop retirement plan. It is the most simple and straightforward approach and what most people consider "traditional retirement." It's got two main components: pensions/government benefits + savings/investments. That's it. For example, let's assume a hypothetical working couple has combined annual household net income (after taxes and savings) of $100,000. If they have Social Security and other pension benefits of $30,000 (net of taxes), they need enough in savings (i.e., their "nest egg") to generate $70,000 after tax per year, rising with inflation, for an assumed thirty-year period. (The Canadian equivalent of Social Security is the Canada Pension Plan (CPP), as well as Old Age Security (OAS) and the Guaranteed Income Supplement (GIS), depending on which of these two you qualify for. To simplify things, we will use the term Social Security even for the Canadian equivalent of CPP/OAS/GIS.)

So how much will they need on day one to finance that level of annual income over a thirty-year retirement? If we assume a 4 percent annual withdrawal rate, they'll need to amass at least $1,750,000 or more to retire. (Historically, 4 percent is a common recommended withdrawal rate for a retiree in their sixties—the amount they can pull from their retirement portfolio and still expect to maintain adequate income and financial independence over the long-term.)

$$\$70,000 = \$1,750,000 \text{ (AFTER TAX)}/0.04$$

If assume that most of the savings is in tax-favored retirement accounts and factor in the taxes payable on withdrawals from these accounts, they'll likely need closer to $2,500,000 in liquid savings and investments.

While the Nest Egg approach is clean and simple, there are a number of reasons why Option 2—the gradual transition of a Victory Lap—is financially attractive and, in our opinion, *superior*. First, it is a Glidepath of income: you continue to earn some level of income while gaining greater control, balance, and enjoyment in life. Financially, this approach to financing retirement is a "three-legged stool" of savings/investments, pension/government benefits, and ongoing active income.

If we use the example of the couple in Option 1, fewer assets are required on day one of a Victory Lap Retirement, because active income will supplement the passive pension/government income and withdrawals from savings and investments. In fact, less savings/investment income will be required in this scenario to reach the annual spending target of $70,000 to cover fixed and discretionary expenses.

Depending on how long we assume this couple will continue to generate active income, and the amount they earn each year in their Victory Lap, the amount of retirement savings prescribed in this scenario could be half of what is needed for the couple choosing the Nest Egg approach at the outset. By extending your earning years and bringing in even a partial income for a period of five, ten, or twenty years, your money will last longer and the financial stability of your retirement plan will improve.

Let's take a closer look at how that shows up over time.

FINANCIAL FLEXIBILITY

In financial planning, we love flexibility. Making permanent or irrevocable decisions that you'll have to live with for thirty years or more is rarely ideal. Think about our concept of retirement twenty to thirty years ago. Many retirees in those days were corporate or government employees who lived entirely on a "fixed income," that is, a fixed pension. Maybe you had parents or family members whose retirement was "fixed" in this way. It likely wasn't a very glamorous lifestyle.

Given the number of unknowns related to markets, interest rates, inflation, taxes, health care, and so on, giving yourself additional flexibility in transitioning to, and living in, retirement is important. Having not "locked in" your retirement chess pieces means you have retained some measure of flexibility to make adjustments as things change. By taking a Victory Lap, you maintain more flexibility and choice over the entirety of your Glidepath and full retirement years. At some point in the future, you could choose to work more or increase distributions from your portfolio to support a family member or take a special family trip. If, on the other hand, you have taken the nest egg approach, you're more likely to be in a "fixed income" mode and less able to make such adjustments or changes to your life when the road has its inevitable twists and turns.

LONGEVITY OF INCOME

Here's the grand-daddy of all financial reasons we think Victory Lap Retirement is so interesting and superior to traditional retirement. In fact, it's the reason we think Victory Lap Retirement will eventually replace traditional retirement and become the dominant path. It's all about the longevity of income, *any* income. This factor makes a huge difference when developing a financial plan. In Rob's experience working with clients, the amount of income, while important, is secondary to the length of it. Why is longevity of income so powerful? Consider these basic concepts. When you generate *any* active income during your Victory Lap:

1. You are reducing the amount you need to withdraw from your retirement "nest egg" to maintain your lifestyle.

2. You are, therefore, allowing your nest egg to continue to grow.

3. You are reducing the number of years of expected future distributions.

4. You might be able to defer pension and government benefits, thereby increasing those benefit amounts in the future.

5. You are diversifying your sources of income and, therefore, are less reliant on the vagaries of interest rates and economic cycles, and on the markets to provide an expected return every year.

The benefits of continuing to generate some level of active income in Victory Lap cannot be understated. Think of it this way: every year that you continue to generate active income in what would otherwise be full retirement, you cause a series of positive benefits to your financial picture.

ACTIVE INCOME AS YOUR PERSONAL PENSION

Corporate pensions are an endangered species due to cost, and the trend toward cutting these traditional employment benefits has accelerated over the last few decades. The idea of replacing your salary, or a portion of it, with some level of active income in Victory Lap can make up for the lack of an employer-sponsored pension plan and takes a lot of stress out of the retirement scenario.

In fact, the active income you earn in your Victory Lap can function much like a pension. Even if this income stream covers only 15 or 20 percent of your overall spending, it is a separate source of income that, although not guaranteed, lessens your dependence on your other sources. People who create this additional income stream have less direct dependence on the performance of their savings and investments and, therefore, are more insulated from fluctuations in interest rates, inflation, economic conditions, geo-political events, and so on—all things that can and will affect returns in your portfolio.

LOWER WITHDRAWAL RATE

If you are earning active income at least for part of your retirement, you can take less out of your nest egg each year and,
therefore, more of it can be reinvested to accumulate and hopefully compound. In the prior example of our hypothetical couple,
any reduction in the $70,000 per year they would otherwise need
to take from savings reduces the stress on the portfolio; they will
not be forced to take money out while markets are down.

One of the biggest challenges for retirees is navigating the
ups and downs of their returns caused by market fluctuations. By
having a lower withdrawal rate for a few years on the front end of
retirement, it's easier to absorb a lower return or even a negative
year or two in the markets. In today's environment, a 2 to 3 percent withdrawal rate is likely to be covered *from the income alone*
(interest and dividends) in your portfolio, as Mike described in
his story on pages 80-81. That is, the sustainably low withdrawal
rate enabled by the active income you earn during a Victory Lap
means you won't have to worry as much about the fluctuations in
your portfolio *value* as you're not depending on capital appreciation, just the *income* from your investments, to supplement your
earned income. This benefit of a Victory Lap should truly allow
you to sleep well at night.

NEST-EGG GROWTH AND HIGHER
FUTURE DISTRIBUTIONS

It follows that if more of the growth component of your portfolio can continue to be reinvested, you can allow more time
for compounding to work in your favor. As a result of earning
some income early in retirement during a Victory Lap, you have
the opportunity to have a much larger nest egg when you do

eventually begin or increase your withdrawals. A larger nest egg affords more safety and/or flexibility in your plan. This flexibility can allow you to increase distributions in the future, decrease the riskiness of the portfolio, or a combination of both.

CHOICE AND PSYCHOLOGICAL PAYOFFS

The psychologically positive impact of nest-egg growth for a retiree is huge. If a sixty-five-year-old retiree walked into Rob's office with a $2 million portfolio and announced that she would like to take out $100,000 every year for the next thirty years from that portfolio, we would likely advise that client to have a portfolio of 60-70 percent in equities in order to provide a high enough return to cover taking out 5 percent per year ($100,000). While doable, this client would be cutting it very close and taking a fair amount of risk in the markets for someone at her age and stage.

We have seen from experience that retirees with that much of their portfolio invested in stocks tend to become obsessive market watchers. They need stocks to provide high single-digit to double-digit returns in *most* years for their plan to work. On the other hand, if that same individual came into Rob's office at age seventy-five, having let that $2 million portfolio grow to $2.5 million, her withdrawal rate would be only 4 percent, and her time horizon twenty years. In those circumstances, she could probably be in a portfolio of 30-40 percent stocks and be able to turn off the market watching and the stress that comes with it!

While we normally have to plan funding for the average two-person, thirty-year retirement, decreasing or delaying distributions in the first ten years of retirement means the liability funding correspondingly shrinks by ten years or more. Now you are funding a twenty-year retirement, which permits an increase in the withdrawal rate when you do start taking distributions.

Whether you choose to increase the withdrawal rate from the portfolio or decrease the riskiness of the portfolio, the active income you earn in a Victory Lap that lasts, say, ten years allows you to secure a measure of flexibility that you can enjoy either way.

PENSIONS AND GOVERNMENT BENEFITS

Taking a Victory Lap means you can continue to have earned income from a business or consulting well into your seventies, which might also allow you to delay triggering Social Security or other pensions until at least age seventy. (An added benefit is that just by delaying Social Security from age sixty-six to seventy, you increase your benefits by 8 percent per year! Similarly, Canadians who defer taking their CPP can increase their payments by 8.4 percent per year.)

If you're taking the Work to Live approach (see chapter 4) and don't need to start receiving your benefits because your cash flow is adequate to cover all your expenses during your Victory Lap, you can continue to let your benefits accrue. When you do stop working completely, you can replace your active earned income with a higher payout than you would have received had you taken Social Security earlier!

Alternately, we occasionally see people taking pensions and/ or Social Security early as a replacement for their salary when following the Passive Income + Playcheck strategy. This works well particularly if the benefits are large relative to your spending, or if your desired Victory Lap pursuit generates lower income or is more hobby-based.

In the Passive Income + Playcheck scenario, it's possible that the income from your pension and/or government benefits can come close to covering your "fixed" spending. With those core monthly needs met, any Victory Lap (earned) income can primarily be used as a supplemental source of funds for discretionary (variable) expenses.

Either way, a Victory Lap strategy can be leveraged to extend your ability to earn active income after you leave your primary career and reduce the draw on savings and investments for a period of years—all while achieving greater work-life balance.

CASHING IN ON LOYALTY

For Rob, two examples come to mind to illustrate some of the principles and benefits we've been discussing. Both are stories of clients, and both were corporate executives with decades of service to a single organization, something that is increasingly rare in today's environment. Dale was a safety expert in the food industry, and Doug was a chemist and researcher for big pharma. Both had accrued sizable pension benefits at work and decided to cut the cord in their mid- to late fifties. With base pensions covering their primary spending needs, both Dale and Doug have leveraged their specialized expertise and extensive professional networks to do consulting engagements and earn supplemental income. One of the main benefits of this strategy is the potential to lower or eliminate withdrawals from their retirement savings.

In Doug's case, he and his wife have been able to live comfortably on his pension and consulting income without taking any funds regularly from their savings over the last ten years. During that time, Doug didn't have to worry about what market fluctuations might do to his distributions as he hasn't had any. As a result, his portfolio has continued to grow substantially. Now in his mid-seventies, whenever Doug decides to stop working (assuming he does), he'll have a considerably larger pile of assets to draw on and fewer years he'll need to provide for, a great financial combo and a recipe that has allowed him to sleep well at night.

Like many consultants taking a Victory Lap, Dale has leveraged a highly respected reputation to build his clientele and income. He first approached us with his pension and said, "Can I be retired? What do I need to make the move?" For Dale, Victory Lap has meant additional freedom. As a hobby farmer raising chickens, growing a large garden, and beekeeping, he's managed to fill his time with his passions while also developing his active income since leaving corporate work a few years ago. Although he wasn't financially ready to retire fully, we developed a plan to help Dale leave his employer and start his Victory Lap. He had an income goal to supplement his pension and serve as a bridge until he takes Social Security.

Dale's first few months were heavy in marketing as he learned that contracts take time and corporate agendas can slow down the process of getting hired and/or paid. Organizations tend not to have the same urgency that any new consultant will to get engagements going. Working out of his home, he's also had a learning curve working with his CPA to determine proper expensing and deductions for his new business. All in all, it's been a fulfilling move that has allowed Dale to begin that Glidepath from the corporate jungle towards full retirement on his own terms.

SAVING NEAR RETIREMENT

Another reason Victory Laps make a lot of financial sense is the diminishing benefit to saving the closer we get to retiring. It's a very simple concept: a dollar saved in your sixties won't have the time to grow and compound as much as a dollar saved in your twenties, thirties, or forties. At a certain point, you might be better off focusing on creating longevity of income versus maximizing what you earn and save in any given year.

Think about it like this: If you save $10,000 into your 401k retirement plan or RRSP in your twenties, it's possible that $10,000 will grow ten-fold by the time you retire at age sixty-five. That's the magic of compounding. If you invested your savings in equities (which have historically provided 8-10 percent total return), you can expect (net of fees) that $10,000 to double in value roughly every ten years. Deposits in your tax-deferred retirement savings that you make in your twenties or thirties have so much time to grow that the value potentially skyrockets, thus $10,000 can turn into $100,000!

In contrast, $10,000 invested in your late fifties or sixties doesn't have as much time to grow because you are so near retirement. While it's always a good idea to save as much as you can, our experience is that it might not be as valuable to stay in a stressful job for the last few years of your career if the main reason you're doing so is the higher income and savings potential. However, if you trade that high income for work that you enjoy and will expect to do for five to ten years longer than you would have been able to tolerate in the higher paying job, you very well may be financially *better off* even though you're voluntarily making less income than you know you can earn in the marketplace.

Several years ago, we had a client who was in corporate sales. Jim made a handsome six-figure living, but work was stressful and required significant travel. When he was between jobs at one point, he presented us with a choice that he had to make. He could pursue a very high-paying job with the prospect of "grinding it out" for five years. He would make enough during that time to save over $50,000 per year more than he had been saving. The other path was to pursue fundraising for his college alma mater. This route meant he would make a lower income but have far less stress, travel less, and have a higher quality of life. As we ran the numbers for Jim, we saw that the increased income and resulting savings in scenario one wasn't going to move the needle on his retirement plan very much at all. However, if Jim were able to work for ten years instead of five in the lower-paying, lower-stress fundraising job, not only would he likely have a better quality of life sooner, but his retirement plan actually projected out better, increasing his financial comfort for the long term. As you can guess, Jim did take the fundraising job, moved back to his home state, and has been working happily ever since.

VICTORY LAP AS RISK MANAGEMENT

A final financial argument for creating a Victory Lap is perhaps the most obvious. With government benefits covering only a portion of most retirees' monthly spending and corporate pensions continuing to disappear, our reliance on retirement savings and investments continues to increase. With that, the dependence on (and, therefore, obsession with) market returns, interest rates, inflation, GDP growth, and other economic indicators is on the rise. We find that retirees are increasingly glued to CNBC to monitor their portfolio and their financial prospects. That's understandable when 70 or 80 percent of your monthly spending seems to depend on what the S&P 500 index does.

While taking a Victory Lap offers the benefit of allowing you to step away from the corporate jungle a few years earlier, it also provides the benefit of *income diversification* right away, and for as long as you continue to have any degree of earned income. Just as diversifying the investments in your portfolio helps to manage risk and maximize returns, having multiple streams of income in retirement helps to do the same thing. The more income sources you have in retirement, there is less chance of you running out of money (longevity risk) and you'll be less dependent on the vagaries of the markets (investment risk).

Another big risk inherent in traditional full-stop retirement is inflation and the loss of purchasing power. At 4 percent inflation, your buying power halves every eighteen years. Retire at sixty-two, and by age eighty your pension will buy half of what it did at that early retirement age. Most seniors today are putting too much of their savings into low-risk investments like GICs or CDs (to try and mitigate investment risk), which means that, with historically low interest rates, they are safely going broke! Continuing to work, at least a little, will enable you to keep topping off your assets, protecting your nest egg from being slowly eroded by inflation.

Less risk overall translates into a more secure and sustainable retirement, and that's better for your pocketbook, your lifestyle, and your peace of mind.

• • •

A successful Victory Lap Retirement *reduces* fear and anxiety. You will benefit from continued earnings over a longer period of time and you will not need to save as much for retirement during your full-time working years, because you are creating a life from which you do not intend to retire anytime soon.

Whether you decide to remain employed to some degree and earn a paycheck, or become self-employed and earn multiple paychecks from a variety of interesting clients, your Victory Lap gives you the satisfaction of staying engaged and fulfilled—all with the peace of mind that you've created a lifestyle for yourself that's meaningful, fun, and sustainable.

6

Putting It All Together

Creating a Financial Plan
for Your Victory Lap

Planning without action is futile, action without planning is fatal.
—*Cornelius Fichtner*

Hopefully at this point you are convinced that a Victory Lap is a compelling idea and worth exploring further. Now is where the real work and fun begin, laying out your plans for making it happen! In this chapter, we'll explore more deeply the financial side of getting yourself prepared to make a move into your Victory Lap. We'll address the key questions you need to answer, potential pitfalls and potholes, and how to take your plan out for a test drive. Let's get started!

TIME TO GET YOUR FINANCIAL HOUSE IN ORDER

In order to hit the finish line of your career job and start your Victory Lap, you have to do some serious planning and preparation to make sure you have your finances in order. After all, you'll want to ensure you're not naively stepping off the proverbial financial cliff to make the move.

It's a surprising fact, but most people do not have a financial plan. Many just rely on the assumption that the more they save for retirement, the better off they will be. While this may seem reasonable, it is not true in all cases. What most people fail to understand is that just achieving a certain level of savings does not guarantee a happy retirement. You cannot assume that because you have a lot of money things will just fall into place when you retire.

PLAN TO SUCCEED

The successful Victory Lappers we have dealt with prepared themselves well in advance and knew the financial pros and cons of what they were embarking on. In our observation, one of the key reasons more people don't take a Victory Lap into retirement is that they are intimidated or downright afraid of looking at their finances for fear of what they might find out. We don't recommend the "head in sand" approach. You need to outline and understand your strategy and how you'll put it into action for success.

So how do you begin to get your financial house in order? It requires some substantial financial planning, ideally with a financial professional (like a CFP, Certified Financial Planner). There is a cost to working with a financial planner, so you'll want to shop carefully for this service and understand the scope of work and fees associated with anyone you're going to engage. You also want to look for a financial adviser who offers a holistic approach and can help with the potential non-financial retirement challenges you may face.

It's true what they say, that the two riskiest years in a person's life are the year they were born and the year they retire. And so it can be of great benefit to have someone to talk to, someone who understands what you are going through and has helped others through it before. Lack of preparedness is often the biggest cause of retirement problems, and good advisers will ensure that their clients are both financially and psychologically prepared for retirement.

If you're not ready to work with a planner or you're more of a do-it-yourselfer, there are a number of financial planning software packages and websites you can consult to get started.

ANSWERING THE BIG QUESTIONS

Regardless of how you choose to go about it, there are a number of significant questions you should address as part of the preparation process. You'll want to make sure you outline and understand the answers to each before you embark on your Victory Lap. Several of these questions may open up other queries and areas to explore. Don't be daunted, though; your health, happiness, and fulfillment are at stake! In short, here are the fundamental questions you should address:

1. What *lifestyle* do you envision for your retirement?
2. What will you need to *spend* in retirement to fund the lifestyle you envision?
3. What is your financial independence *"number"*?
4. Do you still need to *save*?
5. What amount and duration of earned *income* do you need?
6. How will you cover *health care*?

Now let's look at each of these important issues in depth in the sections that follow.

What Good Is Financial Planning Without Lifestyle Planning?

The biggest challenge faced by people who are leaving the full-time workforce is figuring out how they are going to spend the next thirty or more years. Leaving your primary career creates a big void in your life: you now must find ways to fill up the fifty extra hours that have been freed up for you every week. You need to create a plan that is designed to keep you challenged, one that will give meaning to your life and provide satisfaction and a sense of accomplishment while also keeping you fit and healthy. If you fail to come up with a plan to use the leisure time available to you each week, you could suffer from self-doubt, regret, lack of purpose, and boredom.

There's an old saying that most people spend more time every year planning their vacations than their lives. We have always found that to be true. How can you ever know if you have saved enough money if you don't have a good handle on what you want to do in retirement and how much that retirement lifestyle will cost you?

Just remember most retirements fail for non-financial reasons. So be sure that when you're designing a fabulous Victory Lap for yourself, the very first step is figuring out exactly what it is you want out of life once you leave full-time work behind.

If you don't know what you want to do, how can you and/or your adviser possibly figure out how much your Victory Lap lifestyle will cost, and whether or not you are on track to save enough to pay for it?

Joe was happy to hear his financial advisor had passed the new mandatory B.S. detector test.

A good financial adviser will sit down with you and discuss what
you want out of life, then figure out how to build the financial resources to pay for those things that are important to you. Both of
you need to ensure that your life plan is aligned with your financial plan. The key point is that it's *your* own vision based on your
own plans and dreams; *you* need to be the one designing it, it's
not something you can just delegate to your adviser. You need to
hold yourself accountable for planning a successful Victory Lap.

Do You Have a Spending Plan?

How much will you need to, or be able to, spend in retirement?
Many financial advisers like to use an income replacement ratio
to forecast the level of income needed to maintain your lifestyle
in retirement, but really that's just a proxy based on the past.
Your new lifestyle could be completely different from how you
lived previously, which is why you need to take the guess work
out and do a detailed budget and cash flow analysis each year. A
simple ratio will not give you the answer you are looking for.

Will you be relocating? Downsizing? Spending more time on
a hobby? Taking more (or fewer) trips? Your current spending is
a good way to estimate the cost of your lifestyle in the future, but
you'll also want to consider what will be important to you during
your Victory Lap and eventual retirement. This is an area you can't
spend too much time on. You'll want to dig in and really understand
as best you can. It will naturally lead to discussion with your spouse
or significant other about goals and priorities. Schedule time with
your financial planner to review and discuss what level of spending
makes sense in your situation. Discuss it on long drives, schedule a
lunch or dinner conversation with your partner to prioritize what's
most important to you both. Give yourself time to thoughtfully
consider your goals and wishes. Only then can you create an accu-
rate estimate for your level of spending in retirement.

Most people we meet detest doing budgets and avoid them at all costs (which is why we like to call them spending plans). It's ironic that successful people tend to be particularly averse to budgeting. They've generally learned to live within their means and save without getting specific about their spending. This is fine during your high-earning years but won't fly if you're taking a Victory Lap. The reality is, whether you're interested in a Victory Lap or full-blown retirement, a detailed spending plan is simply a must. It is dangerous to embark on any career or life change without understanding your true cost to live.

Once you have a clear lifestyle plan, it's time to convert it to a budget. You need to know what normal monthly and annual outflows are likely to be, including discretionary spending, in order to be certain the strategy you're embarking on makes sense. Break down your spending into fixed (non-negotiable) costs, like rent, mortgage, utilities, insurance, and groceries; and discretionary expenses (eating out, entertainment, travel, etc.). One additional area that people often overlook is non-regular spending. Things like car purchases, roof repairs, and weddings are occasional, but often pricey, line items that you should build into your average spending as well.

This does not, we repeat, *not* require that you do a full forensic audit of your spending for the last three years (phew!). It's about seeing the big picture and getting familiar with the patterns. If you review your bank and credit card statements for six to twelve months, you should see the pattern emerge of your big-ticket items, your regular monthly bills, and your discretionary choices. You'll want to refine it over time, but don't forget to look forward as well. Consider and include the lifestyle planning you've done and factor in how you plan to change your lifestyle (relocate, downsize, etc.) and what that will cost you.

What's Your Number?

Once you've defined the retirement lifestyle you want and corresponding spending plans, the next step is to determine how well funded you are for it. Can you walk away from your job today? Are you on pace to be fully financially independent by the time you want to retire?

A television commercial for a large financial services organization several years ago reduced this exercise to a simple "number." And Lee Eisenberg's book, *The Number: What Do You Need for the Rest of Your Life and What Will It Cost?* is a good primer for this underappreciated subject. Lee's book walks through the calculations required and overlooked line items you should consider when determining your true state of financial independence. While a single number is an oversimplification of the concept of financial independence, solving for it allows you to quantify unemotionally how close you are and identify any gaps. In practice, your number is variable and should be looked at periodically to see if adjustments are needed, even while in retirement.

Working people are often surprised to find out that they're much closer to financial independence than they previously thought. Rob finds that new clients often have great trepidation the first time they create a financial plan together. Mostly, the fear is that they are woefully underfunded for retirement and will be forced to work forever! This is rarely the case, but even if it were true that you are not on the pace you hoped you would be, the sooner you know it and begin doing positive things to change your financial situation, the better.

However you go about the exercise, you're trying to answer a fundamental question: do I have enough income and assets today to retire fully? If the answer is yes, congratulations! You have the ultimate flexibility as you begin to plan your Victory Lap. If earned income is optional for you, you have the freedom to work

on your own terms doing whatever interests you, pursuing a hobby, doing work that helps the greater good, or compensates you
in non-financial ways you care about (socially, passion work, etc.).

Do You Need to Save?

If you haven't quite amassed your recommended "number" yet,
the next question you should answer is, what do I need to save?
How much should I be putting into my retirement savings plans
every year in order to be on pace to accumulate what I project
my number to be? A lot of people are in the fortunate position
of having saved enough, they simply need to let their nest egg
accrue for a few more years.

So when do we have permission to stop saving? For many
hard working, successful people, it's probably sooner than they
think. While there is a looming retirement crisis in our society
because millions have little or nothing saved for retirement, there
are countless "millionaires next door" who have quietly amassed a
seven-figure asset base over the last several decades. Two-income
households in particular have had ample income not only to live
comfortably, but to have saved consistently and often aggressively. Taught by their depression-era parents to save at every turn,
they have. We see them every day, upper-middle-class folks.
They have maxed their contributions to their 401k, IRAs (RRSPs
and TFSAs in Canada), and likely paid down their mortgage in
the process. Having done these things and successfully navigated
the college funding years for children, they have achieved an important footing on the quest to financial independence.

It's very common that these folks have been grinding away,
head down for too long to notice how much they've actually accumulated. I delight in sharing the good news with clients that
they have amassed the nest egg they will likely need (along with
pensions, Social Security, etc.). Often the main ingredient left

for these good people is simply to "let it cook." In dozens of cases over the years, we have concluded that a client five to ten years from a planned retirement is on track, as long as they don't invade their principal in the meantime.

What does this mean? It means, they can afford to reduce or eliminate their savings rate. They have breathing room, and choices. While they likely need to keep working in some fashion to pay their bills and support their monthly lifestyle, the opportunity to lower or eliminate the amount they are regularly contributing to retirement savings can provide some daylight. With that knowledge, they could consider shifting soon into a Victory Lap. These kinds of people are perfect candidates for the "Work to Live" approach detailed earlier.

Even if you haven't amassed quite as large a nest egg, you may still be able to stop saving for retirement when you are just a few years away from that goal, if you intend to earn an active income in your Victory Lap. The "Passive Income + Playcheck" strategy that we also discussed in chapter 4 allows you to cover your fixed expenses by using your pension/government benefits and only the income from your investment portfolio, while using your active income from the work you do in your Victory Lap to finance your discretionary expenses. Yes, you'll have to work at least for a few years at something that you'll get paid for, but you'll be working at something you enjoy and that provides you with a great deal of flexibility and fulfillment—not because you have to, but because you want to.

What Is Your Need for Earned Income?

As you assess your spending needs, how close you are to financial independence, and your readiness to retire and to what degree, you should also arrive at the earned income number you need to target *at a minimum*, in your Victory Lap. It may be 20, 50, or 80 percent of what you make right now in your primary career. Knowing how much income you will need each year (from all sources combined) will guide you in determining what work choices make sense for you in your Victory Lap.

If you need to make only 20 percent of your current income, you might consider the passion/hobby path. On the other hand, if you need to replace 80 percent of today's income, you might be best continuing to do the same work you do now, but repackaging it to be less-than-full-time with an employer or as a consultant (this is the strategy we referred to earlier as Glidepathing).

As you get to this point in the formula, you'll want to be sober and realistic about your options. Balancing risk against your goals and vision is an important part of the conversation. Although leaving your full-time job and benefits to be a Las Vegas lounge singer may be your idea of a dream, it's probably not smart if you still need to keep a six-figure income for a few years!

Now that you've done the math, be honest with yourself about what is realistic. We've seen numerous clients leave the corporate jungle to get into consulting with mixed results. Some were able to secure clients as soon as they walked out the door with their employer, or even before. They had at least one or two "anchor" clients committed to hiring them, thus making the financial transition much easier. Others we've seen were overly optimistic and struggled to convert ideas and leads to business after going out on their own. Be sure to talk to those you trust about your assumptions and plans. See what they think about the viability of your strategy. Factor in how long it might take you to develop your income as you put together your plans. Will the income come all at once or will it build over time? What can you do if it takes longer than you hope to get business? Is there a backup plan?

What Is Your Strategy for Health Care?

It's unfortunate at this juncture that health care is such a costly line item that it needs to be addressed in this book, but if you live in the United States, it's just reality. (This is much less of an issue for Canadian readers, who are covered by universal health care. Still, provincial health plans don't cover everything so you'd be wise to take into account the rising cost of aging, including prescriptions, dental care, private nursing and other health care providers, retirement homes, and long-term-care needs.)

Overcoming inertia is probably the single biggest reason people fail to execute on a Victory Lap retirement; for some, it just feels easier and safer to stay in the corporate jungle rather than to take the leap. Beyond that big challenge, concern about health care is a close second in preventing people from embarking on the freedom and fulfillment of a Victory Lap. Health care is an important wild card that needs to be examined carefully during your preparation for such a move, as not carrying adequate medical coverage can have a devastating effect on your financial plan. If you currently have health insurance through your employer and are under the age of sixty-five (the age you qualify for Medicare), you'll need a plan, especially if you are in the U.S.

In today's market, replacing group coverage with an individual policy can be a major expense. Out-of-pocket expenses continue to rise much faster than basic inflation as well. In financial planning scenarios, we normally break out health care expenses separately and recommend you do so as well. At the very least, factor in the potential for additional costs in your spending and income-generating plans.

The most common solution to this issue? Your spouse. If your spouse plans to continue working and has good group health insurance that you can both access, that may be the easiest and cheapest alternative, especially if you're already on your spouse's plan.

If this is not an option for you, you'll want to do some home-work on purchasing individual health insurance. It's a complicated subject and it's best to talk to a health insurance expert who can help you shop for carriers and policies to price the cost of coverage that makes sense. Either way, once you have your coverage solution outlined, make sure you've added that amount into your planning for expenses and income needed. We recommend creating a sep-arate goal for covering health care prior to age sixty-five (the age U.S. retirees can enroll in Medicare) and normally use a higher rate of inflation for these expenses than other parts of your spending plan, as health care costs have historically risen faster than other areas of spending. This goal should incorporate premiums and any anticipated out-of-pocket costs (deductibles, medication, etc.).

POTENTIAL PITFALLS AND POTHOLES

As you finalize the financial elements of your plans for your Victory Lap, there are a number of things that can adversely af-fect your success. People make mistakes, it's human nature. Here are some of the most common things we've seen in working with clients, and that you should watch out for and avoid.

Beware of Lifestyle Creep

Lifestyle creep can be a problem for people who are getting close to retirement. These people are typically in their peak earning years with corporate perks and an expense account. At this stage in life, it's easy to develop a habit for lavish spending: trips, fan-cy cars, expensive clothing, and paying for someone to clean the house and cut the lawn.

Much of this spending can go unnoticed. For example, some execs have a corporate car allowance and enjoy having a new lux-ury vehicle every few years. This can be a significant expense of $1,000 or more every month for a lease, insurance, etcetera, but it can easily be overlooked when doing a personal budget because it was never a personal expenditure. It's a similar situation with tickets to sporting events, the theater, and other entertainment—a nice perk you get used to and don't account for in your senior position with the Corp, and hard to give up once you leave.

MIKE ON REWARDING YOURSELF

Some of us feel the need to reward ourselves for making it across the finish line of retirement. When I retired from the Corp (for the record, they retired me), I rewarded myself by spending my severance on a new boat, building a "man cave" at the cottage, and purchasing a hot tub.

While the hot tub seemed like a good idea at the time, every time I look at it now I get a headache knowing that we use it only a couple of times a year. Regardless, I still have to maintain it on a regular basis, purchase expensive chemicals, and pay money to have it opened and closed each year. It's a good reminder for me of unnecessary spending. One day I will get rid of it and that will be a blessing!

I'm happy about the boat and man-cave expenditures. We plan on spending a lot of time at the cottage, and now we can accommodate everyone when they come up. It's always a great time when the whole family can get together. I was smart about the boat as well, buying one that wasn't just meant for fishing (one of my passions), but can also take the family out for rides around the lake and pull the kids on their rafts as well.

I'm so lucky I never bought that condo in Costa Rica that I was thinking about. That would have been something else to take care of, and it would have bothered me knowing that I had to go there all the time rather than traveling to other places that I want to visit.

Once you do transition to retirement and start spending more time at home, it is easy to embark on a laundry list of home improvements, particularly renovating your "home office," right? These projects can rack up a significant price tag, yet expenses such as these that were unaccounted for when you created your Victory Lap plan can affect the execution of that plan and the quality of your life, particularly if they go unchecked every year.

Living beyond your means can quickly result in an accelerated drain on your retirement assets and the potential for a declining lifestyle in the future. Lifestyle creep can easily undermine the Victory Lap you've envisioned and put you in a precarious financial position. Keep in mind, most of the overspending that comes with lifestyle creep is discretionary; that is, these expenses were nice-to-have rather than necessary and didn't have to happen. Be mindful of the cost of the finer things in life and choose carefully!

Kids with Their Hands Out

If you have done your job properly, at some point your kids should stop being a drain on your finances. Many parents are happy to help their children out with the cost of post-secondary education, but look forward to the day when they land their first job and start providing for themselves. Unfortunately, this is sometimes not the case. Many parents want their kids to do better and live better than they did, and the unintended consequence is that they have created a sense of entitlement in their children. In some cases, the children don't understand why financial support from their parents should ever stop.

One retiree Mike knows keeps investing in new businesses for his son and they all end up failing. The father was slowly building up the courage to say no, but then his son had kids and he delayed the conversation, at his own peril. It can be even harder to say no when there are grandkids involved, but it still needs to be said.

Some kids view their parents as *their* retirement fund. They don't save for their own retirement and have a lavish lifestyle beyond their means, knowing that one day they will hit the lottery: their inheritance. How does that make *you* feel?

Continuing to provide handouts to your kids (and even planning for a significant legacy to them) may feel like the right thing to do, but it can put a serious wrench in your retirement plans—and it's not doing them any favors in the long run either. It's time for some tough love!

As parents, we need to teach our kids the importance of financial independence and self sufficiency—for their own good, and so that we can have a successful Victory Lap and a rewarding retirement. Your kids need to be resilient and capable of taking care of themselves and their own children. They need to understand how to manage their money, and the importance of gaining financial independence and living within their means.

MIKE'S CAUTIONARY TALE

I was told this sad story by a retirement home operator that I know. The father was widowed and sold his house and moved into an apartment. He gave his kids the money he made from the house sale so they could pay down the mortgage on the large homes that they owned. Let's just say his kids lived well, far better than he ever did in terms of possessions and lifestyle, and his grandkids even went to an expensive private school.

One day the father met some old friends who all happened to live at the same retirement home. The idea of moving to the same community appealed to him so he wouldn't feel so lonely. Unfortunately, he couldn't afford it because his income was too low and his kids couldn't or wouldn't give him back the money he had given them.

Giving large amounts of cash to your children could jeopardize your long-range retirement plans. You are much more than an ATM. Give or lend money only if it is within your means, and if it doesn't prevent you from doing what you want to do and living your own dreams.

The Safe Harbor Principle

Although you may have overcome the urge to provide ongoing financial support to your kids in the form of regular handouts, you may still be called upon to help them in a time of crisis. Sometimes things happen that will force our children to come to us for help, things such as temporary job loss, divorce, etcetera.

It's ok to provide your kids with a safe harbor in times of real need, but don't let them look at you as a permanent source of help. It's fine to allow them to live in the basement for a while until they get back on their feet; just remember to say no when they ask you to buy a new car for them.

MIKE ON HELPING THE KIDS

We all want to help make our kids happy and for them to have a good life. I invested money in my kids' education so that they would have a good start and not begin their working life carrying significant debt. I also spend money on family events and vacations so we can all get together and have some fun. I built the man cave and bought the boat with that in mind, and going forward I plan on helping to fund the grandkids' RESPs (education accounts) so they can get off to a good start as well.

One of the reasons that I continue to work in Victory Lap is to help pay for these family get-togethers because they are so worth it. But that's where I draw the line. After all, I've worked hard all my life so I can enjoy my retirement, too!

Gray Divorce

Divorce rates for seniors, referred to as "gray divorce," are on the rise, roughly doubling in the past twenty-five years for adults ages fifty and older, according to the Pew Research Center. For couples sixty-five and up, it's even worse, roughly tripling since 1990.

Why is relationship breakdown so prevalent at this time of life? Heading into retirement, the kids are gone, your major financial obligations are now behind you, and there is more time for "just us." Unfortunately for some, that extra time together may not be the reward that they thought it would be. Gray divorce is on the rise because people are living longer and they have decided that they don't want to spend all their remaining time being unhappy with a spouse they no longer have anything in common with.

A gray divorce can be as devastating to your retirement plans as it is emotionally. Rob has seen clients go through this many times. As we all know, divorce is expensive and likely results in the splitting up of all your assets. It also requires expert legal and financial advice to avoid paying excessive tax and fees. The end result is typically two bitter ex-spouses, each less well-prepared for their retirement future than if they had stayed married. And with a limited amount of time prior to retirement, it can be very difficult, if not impossible, to recover from the financial hit.

Regardless, it still happens because people see life differently and may have different spending priorities in retirement, which will cause disagreement and stress. Maybe you feel the need for a new car every year while she would rather go to Europe. Maybe you are frugal and he feels the need to buy some new things for the house. Compromises will need to be made if you want to stay happy and married.

To avoid gray divorce you need to have good communication. Make sure you are on the same page, do whatever works for the two of you. And remember, even if you continue to get along famously, everyone needs their own space, their own thing.

Of course, it's also possible that despite earnest efforts, divorce is the best outcome for everyone. In cases like this we hate to see the proceedings get drawn out over a long period of time. As we mentioned above, it's emotionally taxing and leads to a significant erosion of assets, leaving both parties worse off and with little time to recoup for retirement. If parting ways is inevitable, from a financial perspective it is best to make every effort to work together to complete the division of your household and assets so you can both move on. Once that's completed, it is important to build your own financial plan based on your new asset base and financial variables. The sooner you get the divorce behind you and can plan ahead financially, the better.

MIKE ON HAPPY COMPROMISE

I've been through a divorce and believe me I don't want to ever go through that again.

I'm frugal by nature and while that trait has had its benefits, sometimes you just need to respect your partner's wishes and give in, provided that you can afford it. Recently, we did some home renovations and I started out giving the Contessa a hard time about buying some new furniture. I thought what we already had would do, but you don't want your wife looking at her home every day, regretting not buying new furniture so it can look better. So guess what, we have new furniture and I have to admit it looks good. Like they say, happy wife, happy life!

Not Spending Enough Money in Retirement

One of the big challenges retirees face is the major shift in mindset when they switch from savings mode to drawdown mode. After years of frugality and saving aggressively for retirement, many retirees have a hard time changing gears and spending their savings once they get there. They've been so careful to invest for so many years that it just feels wrong to them to spend instead of save. They struggle with paying for vacations, entertainment, going out for dinner, and most other discretionary spending, without generating any earnings to cover it. And this issue is more common that you might think.

A recent Employee Benefit Research Institute study found that people in the U.S. who retired with more than $500,000 in savings still had, on average, 88 percent of it left eighteen years after retirement.

People are overly cautious because they are scared about the future and paralyzed by "what if" syndrome:

- What if we live too long and run out of money?
- What if we get sick and health care costs eat up a substantial part of our retirement assets?
- What if we spend so much that we don't have anything to leave as a legacy for our kids and grandkids?
- What if markets crater in the next month, year, or decade and erode my principal?
- What if the government cuts my pension benefits or raises taxes substantially?

What if, what if, what if?

And because they are scared, they end up playing safe and hanging onto their money. This usually means that they will end up with a lot of regrets over unfulfilled dreams.

The reality is that by the time you are in your late seventies or early eighties you might feel better about not running out of money, but unfortunately you also might be too tired to spend it. At some point you will run out of energy and may not want to go anywhere. Doing the fun things you always thought about doing in your retirement just might feel too difficult by then. Sure, your spending might ramp up again when you lose your health and need to move into a retirement community or nursing home, but good planning well in advance of your actual retirement should account for that increase and allow you to spend in the here and now as well.

Bottom line, it's a big mistake to deny yourself something that you can readily afford when you can best enjoy it. And what is the point of designing an awesome plan for your Victory Lap and, later, full retirement if you're not going to actually live it?

Focusing Exclusively on Preservation of Capital

Regardless of the approach you take to your Victory Lap and the specific strategies you choose to pursue, you want to make sure you structure your portfolio appropriately for both the short and long term. Investors often make mistakes as they switch from accumulation to distribution from their portfolio. The most common is to assume that preservation of principal is now your primary goal. Instead, you'll likely want to have a mix of assets that can provide you both short-term liquidity and long-term growth. In addition to the income (via interest and dividends), you want a buffer of less volatile assets (like cash and high quality bonds) to insulate you from needing to draw against your growth assets (like stocks) during the inevitable periodic market downturn.

As we pointed out in chapter 5, in the longer term you probably don't want to put all of your investments into income or capital preservation assets either. Lots of retirees do this to their own detriment to "protect their nest egg." However, most investors will need a good chunk of growth assets for the long run to continue to have a rising income that can hopefully outpace inflation. We strongly recommend working with your financial planner and/or investment adviser well in advance of your Victory Lap to manage your asset allocation properly.

Not Having a Decumulation Strategy

Now that you know how much money you need on an annual basis, the next challenge is to figure out where to take the money from in a tax-efficient manner. Your single biggest expense in retirement is likely to be taxes, and the method in which you tap your different income streams will have a significant effect on the longevity of your savings.

You need to figure out the optimum timing for starting to draw on each of your multiple income sources, which may include employer pensions, Social Security in the United States or CPP/OAS in Canada, non-registered investment income, annuities, any continuing active income or business income, rental income, and potentially many more.

You also need to give careful thought to when it's best to convert tax-sheltered retirement savings plans like IRAs (or RRSPs in Canada) to income generation; and how to optimize tax-free vehicles like Roth plans (or TFSAs in Canada).

Coordinating all of this is not as simple as merely maximizing each individual stream of income, because tax brackets, clawbacks of government benefits, and other considerations all interact in complex ways. Some of the questions you need to give some serious thought to are as follows:

- Is it more tax-effective to draw down first from regular investment accounts, or from tax-deferred retirement savings/invesment plans?

- Should you delay taking Social Security (CPP in Canada) until age seventy? A similar decision needs to be made for Old Age Security (OAS) in Canada as well. Rob has seen clients continue to earn income from a business or consulting well into their seventies, which allowed them to delay triggering Social Security to age seventy, resulting in a 32 percent increase in benefits.

- Should you also delay taking withdrawals from your IRAs and other retirement accounts until age 70.5 (when required minimum distributions begin), thus preserving the growth and tax deferral of much of your wealth? If you don't need income from these sources right away because you are earning money in your Victory Lap, then your accumulated balances and/or benefits continue to accrue until the time you stop working completely. (Note: IRAs work in a similar way to RRSPs and RRIFs in Canada.)

MIKE ON DECUMULATION

Because I will continue to generate active income in Victory Lap, I plan on deferring taking CPP (the Canadian equivalent to Social Security) until age seventy. The beauty of CPP is that it is fully indexed to inflation, so there are annual increases to cover the cost of living. In addition to that, by waiting to start receiving the benefit at seventy rather than sixty-five, payments to me will increase by an additional 42 percent. Deferring in my case is effective, as I'm transferring some of my investment risk and longevity risk to the government.

In addition, while I will be forced to commence minimum RRIF (Registered Retirement Income Fund) payments when I turn seventy-one (the US equivalent of Required Minimum Distributions or RMDs from 401ks and IRAs that begin at 70.5), I intend to stay fully invested in blue-chip dividend stocks that have a history of consistently increasing their dividends. This strategy offsets the risk of inflation and the possibility of me outliving my retirement assets.

I also am eligible for Old Age Security (OAS) when I turn sixty-five and have the option of deferring it as well to receive higher payments at a later date, but have decided against that. I like the thought of the government paying me at least something sooner rather than later, which I can use to finance my annual fly fishing trip to the George.

The bottom line is that this is complex stuff. If you're unsure as to what to do, you should seriously consider enlisting the help of an adviser.

For readers who would like to learn more on this subject, we recommend reading *The Essential Retirement Guide*, by Frederick Vettese, which applies to both the U.S. and Canada. And for Canadian readers specifically, another book by Frederick Vettese, *Retirement Income for Life*, and *Your Retirement Income Blueprint*, by Daryl Diamond, cover in depth the topics of planning retirement income and decumulation strategies.

TAKE YOUR VICTORY LAP OUT FOR A TEST DRIVE

We test drive many things in our lives, from cars to relationships, before making long-term commitments. So it makes sense to test drive your version of Victory Lap, ideally prior to leaving your primary career, to ensure that it works *for* you rather than *against* you. Victory Lap is a huge unknown, but you can increase the odds of creating an enjoyable one if you spend the time to test it out before actually taking the plunge. We recommend that you start your test period three to five years before you actually leave the Corp behind, with emphasis on the following areas during the test period:

1. Confirm that you can afford your new lifestyle. Test drive living on your Victory Lap budget. Does it meet your expectations?

2. Take a vacation in the location where you plan to reside eventually. If you're going to spend winters in Mexico, test out the community you plan to live in when you're on vacation from the Corp.

3. Try to test your Victory Lap gig. Talk to people already doing it. Try to shadow someone who is doing what you want to be doing in your Victory Lap. Or do your future encore job part-time while you are still in your primary career.

4. Test your future daily routines. Were you bored, exhilarated, overwhelmed?

After a test drive, you will be able to hit the ground running when you start your Victory Lap. You may also be pleasantly surprised to learn that a successful Victory Lap isn't linked to having tons of money, but rather it is linked to living a more interesting, simpler, less expensive and less stressful lifestyle—on your own terms.

SOME RULES TO LIVE BY IN VICTORY LAP

To ensure you have a successful Victory Lap, it's critical to keep both your lifestyle goals and your financial objectives in mind and to plan for them carefully. They go hand in hand at this exciting stage in your life, so don't focus too much on one aspect at the expense of the other. To pull everything together you need to be aware of and address the following:

1. Understand your numbers and live within your means. If you are unsure about the money side, get the help of a financial adviser. Understanding both your financial and lifestyle plan will let you sleep at night and make you less stressed about possibly outliving your money.

2. Your goal should be to maintain your pre-retirement

standard of living. Know what's required and how much income you need to earn to make that happen. It's hard to enjoy retirement if you are being forced to live a reduced lifestyle that you are not accustomed to and don't like.

3. Discuss your financial and lifestyle goals with your spouse/partner to make sure you are both on the same page.

4. Spend more on experiences and less on expensive luxury things. It's all about making great memories and using your time wisely.

5. Victory Laps don't just happen; you need to make yours happen. Have specific plans and goals in place that are in harmony with what you want out of this phase of your life. Have a good reason to get out of bed in the morning. If you don't have specific plans and goals, chances are you will fall into a boring routine, consisting of sleeping in and watching excessive amounts of TV. Don't settle for *Friends* reruns when retirement can be so much more.

6. There will be some bumps in the road at the beginning of your Victory Lap; there always are when you start something new. Understand that it takes time to be really good at something. With practice and experience, things will work out.

7. Inherent in the image of a Victory Lap is a journey, so don't settle for standing still. Keep investing in yourself and never quit learning. Learning is a key element to an

interesting, rewarding Victory Lap: it helps you discover new things; it facilitates you meeting new people with whom you can interact; it provides personal satisfaction and a sense of accomplishment. Be a lifelong learner and challenge yourself every day.

8. Be intentional with your Victory Lap and spend your time wisely. Stay connected with others and remember that curiosity is what keeps you growing. Successful Victory Lappers focus purposefully on growing and maintaining their physical, mental, and spiritual well-being. Failed retirees just take what comes.

9. You don't need to travel the world in order to experience a fulfilling retirement. You can enjoy having a great retirement right in your own backyard. Design the Victory Lap that's right for you.

When you're working full out at a demanding job, it's difficult to be happy because of all the stress that you are under. Once you are able to remove the financial constraints from your life, you will sleep better knowing that you are free to pursue the things that will bring you meaning and happiness. You can do anything for the pure enjoyment of it and take as long as you want to learn, practice, and grow without the pressure to have to make a lot of money from it.

In fact, living a rich life in your Victory Lap is about a lot more than just the financial aspects. We believe that real wealth has a lot more to do with your attitude to money, work, leisure, relationships, and much more. That's why the rest of the book focuses on topics beyond getting your financial house in order;

goal setting, managing your time, and focusing on your physical, mental, and spiritual health are all part of deciding how much is enough at this exciting time of your life.

Now you have the freedom to invest your time in things that excite you, things that you are good at and like doing, things that put you in a state of flow. Designing the Victory Lap that's right for you means that you will no longer allow yourself to be controlled by others, you'll follow your own purpose and take control of every aspect of your own life. Careful, thoughtful planning involves putting all the pieces in place to make sure that the Victory Lap you envision actually happens. And we bet that you'll be all the happier for it!

7

Goal Setting and the Pursuit of Happiness

Are You Aligned?

The best way to predict the future is to create it.
—Abraham Lincoln

If you do what you've always done, you'll get what you've always gotten.
—Anthony Robbins

The quote above by Abraham Lincoln is something of which we should all remind ourselves every day. We all have the power within us to control our destiny, but we often forget this as we become overwhelmed by life's complexities. We're so busy with day-to-day living that we don't have time to stop and think about what we really want out of our life and how we can make our dreams a reality. We assume that if we go to work, follow orders, and work hard, everything will work out in the end, but this is one of the biggest mistakes we can make.

Many people allow their lives simply to happen to them, focusing only on getting through the next day, week, or month. Years fly by and valuable time is wasted, until the day they eventually wake up and wish they had taken charge of their life and set goals earlier. To avoid this from happening to you, you need to know what you want out of life, then figure out a way to get there. That goes as much for planning your retirement as it does for any other time in your life, although it's arguably even more important when planning your Victory Lap, to ensure you avoid drifting aimlessly through your later years. When you have a full-time job, goals and structure are imposed on you even if you don't create them for yourself. When that employment suddenly ends, you have to set your own goals and structure your life for yourself.

Setting goals restores a sense of focus in a world that has become complicated by too many options and distractions, and it provides a sense of purpose, particularly for those faced with the blank slate of retirement. Goals clarify our desires and help us focus on those activities that will lead us to where we want to go. Goals and plans take the worry and stress out of living: you'll know exactly where you want to go and how you'll get there because you have a plan aligned with your objectives. Goals commit you to a course of action. Setting goals that engage and motivate you is one of the best ways to boost the level of your personal commitment to life and bring energy to your days.

Happiness comes from knowing where you want to go and why, setting worthy goals, and achieving them as you follow the game plan for your life. Happiness comes from knowing that you gave life your best shot!

FAILING TO PLAN IS PLANNING TO FAIL

Those who set goals and prepare plans to achieve them succeed in life. Setting a goal and not creating and following a plan to achieve it is merely a wish. Hope is not a strategy; a well-thought-out plan is. Following are some recommended steps that will help guide you in planning your Victory Lap goals.

Step 1: Articulate Your Dream for Victory Lap

The first step is to articulate your vision for your own personal Victory Lap, one that will allow you to live the longest, healthiest, most interesting, and most satisfying life that you can. All of your dreams and goals must be aligned with what you want to accomplish in life and with what you wish to become.

Once you have determined what you are passionate about, you need to make your goals come alive in your imagination.

Visualize exactly what you want to do and where you want to go. The more vivid the image, the stronger your desire to get there will be. Our vision delivers to us our *ikigai*, or reason why we get out of bed each morning. Dream large and feel your happiness and energy start to flow.

Step 2: Establish Your Core Goals

Core goals are themes that form the code you choose to live by in order to achieve your vision. Think about the accomplishments you would want talked about in your eulogy: "She loved life," "He cared and always put his family first," "He was a generous man." Visualize your legacy after you're gone and how those who survive you will describe that legacy: how you had helped others, showed compassion, and made contributions to your community.

Core goals are based on what a person wants to accomplish in life, not in terms of making money or acquiring more stuff, but how you can help and touch the souls of others.

Step 3: Establish Your Short-term Goals

Short-term goals serve as stepping stones that help us realize our long-term vision for a healthy Victory Lap lifestyle. From longevity studies we know which areas in our lives we need to address—the things we need to do to keep engaged, healthy, and balanced. We need to take that knowledge and convert it into clear and well-defined sub-goals so that we, too, can live a long life.

These short-term goals will become the "how," the steps you will take to achieve the bigger vision you have of the kind of Victory Lap you want to run. The key in establishing short-term goals is to make sure they are clearly articulated: write them down, set a specific completion date, and hold yourself accountable.

Examples of short-term goals include:

- Achieve financial independence by December 31, 2020
- Meditate for thirty minutes each morning commencing February 1, 2019
- Lose thirty pounds by December 31, 2019
- Restrict television viewing to one hour a day commencing April 1, 2019
- Volunteer to help organize the local hospital charity run on April 1, 2020

Tracking your progress on a spreadsheet and regularly comparing it with your goals will serve to motivate you and ensure that you stay on track. The real value of setting and achieving goals lies not so much in the rewards you receive but *in the person you become* as a result of reaching your goals. Celebrate the fact that the process of reaching your short-term goal has improved the person that you are. You have built self-discipline, discovered new things about yourself, and realized more of your human potential. Not a bad deal! And as you begin achieving the goals you've set for yourself, continue to develop new ones. Remember, your Victory Lap is a purposeful journey—don't stand still.

THE ANNUAL REVIEW

Every year between Christmas and New Year's, Mike and the Contessa sit down and review their personalized "road map," the goals they set for themselves annually. This road map is broken down into a number of categories: health, family, money, experiences, top ten list, good/bad habits, and so on. They review the goals they have accomplished over the past year and establish new goals to ensure continual progress toward their ultimate goal of "an awesome Victory Lap lifestyle." They make a list of the special events that will be coming up—birthdays, anniversaries, special occasions, holidays—and plan ways to make them unique and memorable. Family experiences are where you want to invest your time. The payback in terms of personal satisfaction is huge!

Here's an example of how Mike set short-term goals that aligned with one of his major objectives: to help people through sharing advice and offering encouragement and hope in his writing (both through this book and his blog). As Malcolm Gladwell posits in his book *Outliers: The Story of Success*, it takes approximately 10,000 hours to become a master at anything. Based on this idea, Mike calculated that the realization of his major goal would take him on a journey over a ten-year period. Following are the short-term goals he plans to meet to help him get there:

1. To stay productive over those ten years, he established fitness and nutritional goals to ensure he would remain healthy and maintain high energy during that period.
2. To create awareness of the concept behind Victory Lap, Mike established the goal of having the original edition of *Victory Lap Retirement* completed and ready for edit by June 2016.
3. He joined the local chapter of Toastmasters International, which would help when it came time to market the book and speak at seminars about it.
4. Mike also set a goal of writing blogs for other retirement sites in order to help create even more awareness for the book.

To live well and succeed in life you need to be intentional, purposeful, and work continually toward a worthy goal that you set for yourself. You can't expect a positive outcome if you don't have a viable plan. Without goals you're at the mercy of whatever happens. The simple truth is that successful people succeed because they know where they want to go and how to get there.

ALIGNING DAILY HABITS WITH LONG-TERM GOALS

We are what we repeatedly do. Excellence then, is not an action, but a habit.
—Aristotle

Motivation is what gets you going. Habit is what keeps you going.
—Jim Rohn

The goals we set for ourselves are important drivers, motivating us to achieve the big things we want out of life. So it's amazing to note that, according to the results of a Duke University study conducted in 2006, more than 40 percent of our days are actually controlled by habits and routines that we have created for ourselves over the years. Over time, habits become part of our daily rituals and we are no longer conscious of the routine being carried out. Habits and routines cause us to do things the same way every day.

Think about when you take a shower and the routine you have developed over the years. Your routine is carried out without conscious thought; but see what happens when you disrupt the pattern by thinking about something else while you are performing the task. How many times has this happened to you? You can't remember whether you shampooed your hair or not because your normal routine, which is usually on autopilot, was disrupted by some distracting thought that entered your mind. The fact is that most of us are on autopilot for most of the day.

Whereas goal setting is intentional and can lead to feelings of accomplishment, purpose, and fulfillment, habits are unconscious and automatic; they control our daily lives to a great degree, which can lead to boredom, aimlessness, apathy, general unease, and sometimes much more unhealthy consequences.

Of course, there are good habits and there are bad habits. Most of the time it's pretty easy to tell them apart and to know which ones you ought to adopt and which ones you should stay away from. For instance, you know that eating multiple servings of fruits and vegetables every day is a good habit to get into, and that smoking is a habit you should break or avoid. But even good or benign habits can lead you astray if they are not aligned with your long-term goals and if they are not intentional.

The thing is, you're unlikely to achieve a goal unless your habits support it. Therefore, if your existing daily habits are not aligned with your long-term goal, you'll need to change your habits in order to reach your goal. When you set a goal, think about what habits you need to change or what would allow you to put the obtainment of that goal on autopilot. For instance, if you wanted to save a certain amount of money to take a much-needed vacation, you might consider eliminating your "retail therapy" habit of walking the malls on the weekend. Or instead of going out for an expensive lunch every day of the week, perhaps you choose to bring a healthy lunch to work. You will end up saving lots of money and getting healthier at the same time.

Adopting and maintaining good habits is hard enough at the best of times, and harder still when you're surrounded by the noise of advertisers tempting you in their direction. Consumer marketers spend millions upon millions of dollars studying the effect of habits, using what they learn to help them market the tons of (largely unnecessary) products we consume every year. They understand how the average person responds to the marketing of luxury products, and they use this information to try to trap us in a habitual purchasing routine. In other words, they put a spell over you and turn your family into consumer zombies.

Advertisers know that most of us are unwilling to spend much time and effort on something after we've endured another long, hard day at the office. Why do you think they created mail-in rebate programs? They know many of us will not expend the energy to mail in the rebates, even though it means saving money. How dumb (or smart) is that? Advertisers know our own habits better than we do.

That's why it's important to fully understand the power that your habits hold over you and to find ways to change them so you

Within a few short months of retiring,
Mike started to look like Howard Hughes...

can regain control over your life. Unbeknownst to you, habits will take you in a particular direction—potentially one you do not really wish to go in—so it's important to ensure that your habits are aligned with your dreams. Choose your habits intentionally, or they will choose your destiny for you.

Over time, habits become automatic and take little effort, so you don't need to think much about what you are doing. This is fine if the habit in question is healthy, but if it's a negative habit it could destroy you if it continues long enough. According to the 2012 *Medscape Physician Lifestyle Report*, 44 percent of doctors are overweight, even though they are well aware of the importance of regular exercise and good nutrition. Knowing what to do is meaningless if you are unwilling to spend the effort and put the right habits in place.

Changing a habit is often easier said than done, as it takes a certain amount of self-discipline. In his book *The Power of Habit: Why We Do What We Do in Life and Business*, Charles Duhigg reveals ways to help change these powerful routines. Habits start with a trigger and end with a reward that reinforces the habit. The best way to change a habit is to keep the same trigger and reward but change the pattern in between. According to Duhigg, here are some steps you should take to invoke habit change:

1. **Determine the trigger for your habit.** For instance, say you have developed the habit of drinking a beer or two while you barbeque your dinner. The habit of having a beer is triggered by the lighting of the barbecue.

2. **Use the same trigger, but replace the routine with a different behavior.** So instead of opening a beer after lighting the barbecue, you could talk to your family and

see how their day went or you could pick some weeds out of the garden or water your lawn.

3. **Keep the reward similar to the old one.** After having a beer you feel relaxed, so make sure after you barbecue that you sit down and decompress however you want. Instead of a beer, enjoy a coffee or perhaps an iced tea.

The key is to understand your habits and how they control your life. Awareness will allow you to find ways to create positive change. Always be aware of what is happening around you, why it's happening, and how it can impact you. Stay in the moment, be aware of it, and you will be much better off for it.

A useful exercise is to list all the bad things that could happen if you don't change the bad habits, then list all the good things that will occur if you make the required changes. When you start with the end in mind, it's easier to analyze each choice closely and make the smart choice so you can achieve your goals.

Once you create a habit, good or bad, over time that habit starts to control you. It's important to understand that habits are not temporary; it becomes very difficult to delete a programmed behavior. You must strive to adopt only habits that in the long run will be beneficial rather than destructive to you. Your quality of life will be determined in large measure by the nature of your habits. The key is to ensure that your habits move you forward rather than hold you back. For example, you know you need to institute proper lifestyle habits in order to meet the goal of increased longevity. And so you must get in the habit of eating right, exercising, and socializing regularly with family and friends. The bottom line is that you need to be intentional and create everyday habits aligned with your long-term goals.

MIKE'S CHANGING HABITS

I was concerned when I set the long-term goal of having an amazing and fulfilling Victory Lap that there were certain habits in my life that were working against my goal. I am in the process of trying to change these habits for the better, to ensure that my Victory Lap is vibrant, rewarding, sustainable, and fun.

1. **Exercise:** Because I want to enjoy a healthy life for as long as possible, I needed to adopt a more active lifestyle. Recently I started to walk outdoors with the Contessa; the game plan is to transition into a walk/run program with the ultimate goal of completing a half marathon.

   Also, instead of driving everywhere, I plan on biking whenever possible, whether to the gym, library, or shopping mall. By adopting a disciplined exercise program I will lose weight, gain energy, and hopefully get myself off the blood pressure pills I have been taking.

2. **Nutrition:** I've always been a meat-and-potatoes guy and there has never been much room on my plate for vegetables or other healthy foods. But I have awoken to the evil of my ways and decided to work hard in this area. More fish, salad, and fruit and less booze. Besides the money we'll save, the health benefits are priceless.

3. **Time:** Watching television, especially NFL football, was my way to decompress after a hard day or week at work. Over the years, it's surprising just how much time is wasted watching mindless TV (whether sports, reality TV, game shows, or much of the other drivel that passes for "entertainment" on the tube). When you add social

media (e.g., Facebook, Twitter, Snapchat) the numbers are frightening.

There is only so much time in the day and to waste a major portion of it on non-productive activities doesn't make a lot of sense. TV is the easy choice, the path of least resistance for many of us. Do what I have done and replace the TV/internet habit with reading and exercising more. Through watching TV we fill our minds with so many negative things, and now I feel much more positive about things. Not a bad trade-off!

HABITS AND THE POWER OF COMPOUNDING

Compound interest is the eighth wonder of the world. He who understands it, earns it. He who doesn't, pays it.
—Albert Einstein

Ask your financial adviser about the most important rule to follow in order to grow wealth, and she or he will undoubtedly talk about the power of compounding and diversification. When you put the power of compounding to work for you, your money will grow at exponential rates. That's the positive side, but the power of compounding can also work against you.

Even a harmless little habit, such as going to Starbucks, Dunkin' Donuts or Tim Hortons every morning, can translate into big money thanks to the magic of compounding. For example, Mike has developed the habit of visiting Tim's most days, and he spends at least $5 every time. If instead of spending this $5 he had invested it at a 6 percent return, over the course of twenty years he would end up saving close to $70,000. In other words, that daily Tim's run will end up costing Mike $70,000. Is the coffee at Tim's really that good? Wouldn't Mike be much better off just making his own coffee and toast at home?

Cutting back on visits to the coffee shop is just one example of how we can take action to reduce the "habit interest" that costs us a lot of money over time. Other examples are your cable bill, cell phone bill, internet bill, buying books frequently instead of going to a library, and even activities that are as destructive to your health as to your pocketbook, cigarettes being the obvious example.

Every time you eliminate frivolous expenses, the power of compounding will eventually turn every penny saved into nickels, and if invested properly over the long run, the nickels will grow into dimes, quarters, and so on. The thing to understand is that if you do something small repeatedly, the benefits or costs will accrue exponentially over time. Whether that effect is negative or positive is based on choices we make every day.

This rule applies outside finance too. Let's use health as an example. Mr. A is a successful executive who works hard but is so stressed out at the end of the day that he needs to decompress by sitting in front of the TV for the evening, munching on potato chips and enjoying a beer or three. By contrast, Mr. B has a similar job, but he decompresses by going to the gym a few times a week. He also goes for a nice stroll with his wife after dinner each night. Now imagine whose shoes you would rather be in after twenty years of these habits. Here's a clue: we hope you didn't pick Mr. A because he might have died from a heart attack by then!

Victory Lap gives all of us a chance to write our own story. We need to be intentional with the rest of our lives through goal setting and the adoption of good habits and routines. Solid financial and lifestyle habits should be based on an understanding of what will happen in the long term because of them. If we change our bad habits, we can change our future and improve our chances for a much happier ending. Identify those little habits that are holding you back and replace them with good ones. Always remember that tiny successes achieved each day will compound into large successes over time.

Time as a Resource

Every Day Matters

Time is more valuable than money. You can get more money, but you cannot get more time.
—*Jim Rohn*

A chieving financial independence means you have earned the freedom (time) to spend your days as you please. This is potentially liberating, but you have to ensure that you don't waste time; it is all too fleeting and you will one day realize that a shortage of time will start to eliminate opportunities rather than create new ones. Eventually your physical abilities, and ultimately your mental faculties, will start to diminish and your options will begin to narrow. The key is to recognize time for what it is, so you can maximize its use and avoid any regrets down the road.

After losing his keys, Jonathan had to be
more careful about how he used his time.

The good news is that if you were able to juggle your time and
priorities successfully when you were in the Corp, it should be a
snap to achieve a satisfying work-life balance once you start your
Victory Lap. Remember, you have the same twenty-four hours
per day that Bill Gates, Warren Buffett, Prem Watsa, Ian Telfer,
and Mark Zuckerberg have. How do you plan on spending yours?
The most important decision you make each day is how you will
invest your time. There's a Mark Twain quotation we refer to
later in the book, and it's fitting to mention here also: "Twenty
years from now you will be more disappointed by the things you
didn't do than by the things you did do."

By effectively managing your time in Victory Lap you can
create one of the most fulfilling and inspiring periods of your life.

The freedom you'll experience in this unique phase will allow you to customize a work-life balance that works specifically for you. And soon you'll come to realize that, yes, you can have it all!

TIME, MONEY, AND LIFE ENERGY

One thing you discover early in the experience of a Victory Lap is the fluidity of time and its continued connection to money. It's a common observation that "time is money," but the corollary is also valid: "Money is time."

During the years of working toward financial independence, you are trading time for money, which amounts to transforming your human capital into financial capital that can be used in the distant future. As we all know, a young person just entering the workforce has potentially millions of dollars' worth of *human* capital ready to deploy but very little in the way of *financial* capital.

As the decades progress toward financial independence, this human capital starts to decrease, even as financial capital grows. In the old construct called full-stop retirement, the ultimate aim was to have enough financial capital in old age that it would no longer be necessary to use any of your human capital to generate money. No matter how you envision your retirement years, you just can't count indefinitely on your human capital to be available to convert into wealth. That's why the financial institutions are constantly nagging us to save for retirement.

Closely connected to the concepts of human capital, financial capital, time, and money is the idea of life energy. We all have a certain amount of spiritual essence or life force. When we take on a physical or mental task, some of this energy is expended, and we know, too, that we eat and sleep to recharge this energy. Like our time, it appears that our life energy is also a finite resource.

One of the classic books on financial independence is devoted to the interplay between life energy and money: *Your Money or Your Life: Transforming Your Relationship with Money and Achieving Financial Independence*, by Joe Dominguez and Vicki Robin. Dominguez retired from Wall Street at age thirty-one and never again accepted money for any work he did.

A key concept in the book is that money is something for which we choose to trade our life energy. Every time you deploy life energy (part of which is your time) on a money-creating task, realize that you have that much less life energy left for the future. Life energy is precious because it is finite and, once expended, is gone forever. If the task you performed resulted in payment in the form of money, you need to view that money as, in essence, a tiny portion of your personal life energy.

Of course, life energy can be expended on other things than generating money, even though full-time jobs in our primary careers do tend to consume about one-third of our waking time (and a lot of our life energy). Life energy is also expended on non–money-generating activities, such as cultivating relationships with family and friends, volunteering in the community, and purely "fun" leisure activities that are more apt to consume amounts of money rather than bring in money.

Charles Sharun is a friend of ours whose day job was as a painter of sets in the film business. He moved to the country in his late sixties in order to pursue his dream of becoming a full-time artist. But even before he made the move, he would build small stakes in the lucrative film business, then take chunks of time off in order to focus on his dream. Charles calls this "buying time." By working hard for six months at a time on one or two major film projects, in return he was able to save up enough money to "buy" six months of precious time to devote to his art.

Looking at it from this perspective, money is precious, assuming you agree that your life energy is also precious. So when it comes time to spend the money, you need to view its possible expenditure as the equivalent of dissipating your personal life energy. It's fine if the expenditure is a worthwhile one: either a cherished life experience (e.g., travel, education, time with family) or an item of consumption that enhances your physical well-being (e.g., nutritious food, smart clothes that make you employable, a roof over your head). But the flip side of spending money, and hence expending some of your life energy, comes when you in essence "waste" that money. We've all done so at some point in our lives: perhaps buying an exercise bike that never gets used beyond being a handy place to throw your clothes, blowing money at a casino, or taking a flyer on a speculative penny stock or a so-called blue chip like Nortel that promptly falls to zero. In all these cases, you end up with nothing to show for your expenditure of money and, therefore, nothing to show for the life energy you spent to accumulate that money. You have "wasted" not just your time but also your limited life energy and the money into which that time and energy was transformed.

THERE'S REALLY ONLY ONE DAY: DON'T WASTE IT

If you believe that life energy is precious, then so is the time you have available to expend life energy. When we enter this life, we're all given the same deal: each day we live has only twenty-four hours, and not even a billionaire can turn that twenty-four hours into one hour more. Henry Blodget once devoted his column at *Business Insider* to this very topic. He noted that most humans get about seventy-five years of existence on this planet, which translates into 3,900 weeks, the equivalent of approximately 27,000 days, or 648,000 hours.

When we saw that number—648,000 hours—we were astonished. That's not a lot of time, and it's a remarkably finite figure. Those of us fortunate enough to accumulate $648,000 probably don't view such a sum of money as infinite; we're well aware of how fast it could be depleted over a long retirement. So isn't the amount of 648,000 hours just as finite?

Suddenly, those sixteen hours of the twenty-four-hour day that we call "waking time" become even more precious. In each week, you have a total of 168 hours—only 112 if you consider that you "lose," on average, fifty-six hours to sleeping. Blodget observed that 150 years ago, seventy of those 112 waking hours were spent working. Today, thanks to the productivity-enhancing effects of technology, the average workweek in most countries has dropped by about thirty hours. Sadly, and this has profound implications for our Victory Lap concept, we spend most of that extra time watching television. According to research done by The Nielsen Company, Americans spend on average a whopping four hours a day watching TV, or twenty-eight hours a week.

A follow-up to Blodget's column was done by *Business Insider*'s Andy Kiersz in mid-2015, and he found slightly different statistics from the 2014 American Time Use survey. Based on that information, sleep continues to account for the biggest slice of the day: 8.8 hours on average, or eight hours and forty-eight minutes. When it came to work and work-related activities, because the survey participants included the unemployed or "retired," who would have spent zero hours a day working, this brought down the overall average and offset the normal eight hours that most full-time workers spend, but these activities still came second, accounting for an average of 3.59 hours. We'll round it up to four working hours, which is pretty significant. Watching TV accounted for 2.82 hours a day, while household activities made up 1.77 hours, leisure activities (other than watching TV) 1.48 hours and—get this—eating and drinking accounted for 1.17 hours. Personal care or grooming was 0.78 hours, educational activities were a tiny 0.42 hours a day, and exercise was an even tinier 0.29 hours.

To get a reality check on how limited our hours are on this planet, we recommend you watch a three-minute video on YouTube that really brings the point home: https://www.youtube.com/watch?v=BOksW_NabEk. Or just google "You have 28,835 days. Here's how you will spend them." The video shows 28,835 jelly beans, each one signifying a day of your life. Of course, the fortunate will have more than 28,835 days in their lives; the unfortunate will have less, but 28,835 is the average on which the video is based.

Our main premise—and we'll concede it's a mental concept, albeit a useful one—is that "There's only one day." If you accept this, it follows that every day matters and should not be squandered. For most human beings the day consists of sixteen hours, the other eight being given over to sleep. We acknowledge that there are some who extract eighteen or twenty hours or more of productivity in their day by going with less sleep, but for the purpose of argument, let's agree on a sixteen-hour day. Now consider that everything you see on earth, from the pyramids to the CN Tower, the greatest corporation, the longest novel, and the most stirring symphony was created by human beings in a series of sixteen-hour days, or more likely eight- or nine-hour days. Yes, big projects require the stringing together of hundreds or perhaps thousands of days, but the basic unit is the single day. That day has a structure that is replicated over weeks, months, and years.

For an office worker, the structure of a single working day is very familiar. While there may be various internal and external meetings on different days so that, superficially, each day will appear somewhat unique, in a given week Monday, Tuesday, Wednesday, Thursday, and Friday will unfold in pretty much the same way for the worker: waking at a certain hour, commuting to the office to arrive by 9 a.m., experiencing a whir of activity or meetings followed by lunch, experiencing another whir until about 5 p.m., then commuting home, and so it goes.

When you leave the structure of the office workday for Victory Lap Retirement, your success or failure during this stage will depend largely on how you approach the structure of the basic template for every day. The key to creating an effective template for your typical day is to recognize how mental and physical energy ebbs and flows over the day, and to build that into a structure for the model day that works for you.

HOW TO WORK JUST FOUR HOURS A DAY

If there's one thing Victory Lap provides, it's time freedom. No longer shackled to the eight-hour day of the Corp, you're free to practice something called "the four-hour workday." As you'll see, it's also possible to adapt this concept while you're still in the Corp: you can build a high-intensity four-hour day into the average eight-hour day, and that day can be repeated over and over again, with variations and accommodations that adapt to particular changing circumstances.

The idea for the four-hour workday originated in the 1950s, when William J. Reilly wrote a book called *How to Make Your Living in Four Hours a Day Without Feeling Guilty About It*. Reilly pointed out that when you look at very highly creative people, such as composers, novelists, or even high-level executives, they really have only four or five hours of high-level mental energy available daily to perform the tasks they have to do, and very few general types of workers expend high energy for every hour of their eight-hour workday.

For senior managers and creative types, what's important is the high-level brainpower being expended, not the amount of time one's bum adheres to an office chair. So it's important, whether you're a salesperson, executive, artist, musician, or writer, to spend at least two hours of the workday morning doing the work you're really paid for: making cold calls or closing deals if you're in sales, writing articles if you're a writer, writing a symphony if you're a composer, and so on. Having done your two-hour morning stint, you're then free to spend two hours over lunch networking, learning, or exercising, as long as you promise yourself to spend at least two hours in the afternoon doing the work you're really paid to do.

Of course, most corporations like to see plenty of face time from their employees, preferably from 9 to 5. And so, if you're still in the Corp you may have to resort to a compromise, which is a four-hour day tucked inside the eight-hour office day. As an example, imagine that your morning shift of "real work" is between 10 a.m. and noon and that the afternoon shift is between 2 and 4 p.m. Both involve being at your desk making sales calls, editing, writing, budgeting, or whatever. Note that this leaves an hour both first thing in the morning and at the end of the day for doing things like reading the paper, dealing with email, or checking social media. It's perfectly fine to "gear up" in the first hour or two of the corporate day and "wind down" toward the end, just so long as you get the "real" four hours of high-level brain activity done. It's that activity, after all, for which you're getting paid the big bucks.

ROB ON THE MYSTERY OF T2T

About ten years ago I was fortunate to meet one of the great personalities I've ever come in contact with. Hank was a family steward in his eighties at the time. A child of the Depression, he was a successful, self-made businessman and taking care of his family was the most important thing to him in life. He'd had a number of careers over the decades and was in sales when I met him. That's right, he was still working in his eighties. In fact, he gave me his business card. Along with all the usual contact information, it had his name centered with an important title below it:

HANK
T2T

T: 123.456.7890
E: contact_hank@t2t.com

When I asked Hank what T2T stood for, he grinned and said, "You don't know what T2T is?" I assured him I didn't, and he laughed and said I wasn't old enough to understand. Pausing, he said he and his friends all "work T2T: Tuesday to Thursday from 10-2," then he let out a bellow and sat back in his chair. We both laughed and he further described that he consistently worked in his home office, making calls and touching base with his network during those hours. It was part of his social existence and he couldn't see himself ever giving it up. Truth be told, I don't know how much income Hank really made from his T2T activity, but that's not the point. He had a community he enjoyed staying connected with in this way and he embraced staying plugged in part-time, from T2T. I often think about how lucky we'd all be to feel productive and engaged in the same way into our eighties, especially if we were able to do it T2T!

The corollary of "There's only one day" is "Every day matters." No matter how large the tasks are before you, you can only tackle them one day at a time. If you deploy your life energy on the important tasks each and every day, you can be sure your goals will be achieved. You know what they say about how you eat an elephant: one bite at a time. Waste a precious day of what we call "Monday to Friday time," and you've lost a bit of momentum.

Going back to the YouTube jelly bean video, we are creatures assigned 20,000 or 30,000 days on this planet, with each of those days made up of twenty-four hours, no more no less. The hour allotted to the billionaire is no longer than the hour experienced by a panhandler. How you choose to spend those twenty-four hours makes all the difference in your life.

MAKE THE MOST OF EVERY DAY
IN YOUR VICTORY LAP

As any financial planner can tell you, if you knew precisely the date of your demise, it would be a simple matter to calculate how much money you could safely withdraw from your portfolios each year during retirement. You wouldn't have to worry about when your money would run out because you'd plan for it to run out a few days after you were buried. You know the old joke: The last check you write should be to your undertaker, and it should bounce! Of course, being the considerate person that you are, in actual fact you would arrange a prepaid funeral to spare your heirs the expense.

Unfortunately (or perhaps fortunately, depending how you look at it), we generally do *not* have advance knowledge of our death day. We all hope it's thirty or forty or more years from now, but of course it's quite possible that today will turn out to be our last day. This is why there's some wisdom in the saying that we should live as if every day is our last day on earth, because one day it will be. This is another reason that we are inspired to adapt Richard Bolles' *Three Boxes of Life* concept, of incorporating at least an hour or two of leisure, learning, and satisfying work into each day. This is easier to achieve in your Victory Lap than at any other time in your life. This special period allows you to achieve the kind of balance in your life that you can only dream about during any other time.

Think how sad it would be to spend your youth entirely at school learning and your middle years entirely at work, and then die prematurely just as your golden years of leisure were about to begin. Tragically, we see this all the time: money-oriented top executives or entrepreneurs who work around the clock in the sole pursuit of a large sum of money that will supposedly enable them to move from 100 percent work mode to 100 percent leisure mode at the right moment. It's largely a pipe dream and the basis for the popular saying (usually by those not so driven), "I don't want to be the richest man in the cemetery."

Lots of Rob's clients continue to work beyond the point of achieving financial independence, often because they simply enjoy the work and the people too much to leave. We just don't want to see them lose precious time because they don't know how to change or they simply procrastinate. It's unfortunate, but we've seen clients who could have retired years earlier get a devastating diagnosis for themselves, their spouse, or another loved one, that cuts time short. In those instances, we'd all do anything to turn back the clock and give that individual or family precious months or years back but, of course, we can't.

Back to Bolles, it's far better, we think, to mix up the boxes a bit so that they're non-sequential in your life and spread more evenly throughout your lifespan. That is, taking a Victory Lap allows you to play a little more in your earning years (taking some of your retirement, or at least more leisure time, a little early).

Victory Lap also lets you work a little in your life beyond full-time employment, earning a little "fun" money while keeping you more stimulated, challenged, and active than a life of unending leisure would. Taking a Victory Lap can introduce more balance into your life not only each and every day that you are running that Victory Lap, living a new kind of retirement, but also throughout your life, as you redistribute your work, leisure, and retirement time.

By living life this way, you will benefit from thousands of hours of learning, earning, and leisure, all experienced in the now of each day, the only day there really is.

9

Health Is Wealth

We do not stop playing because we get old; we grow old
because we stop playing.
  —*George Bernard Shaw*

G iven the financial focus of this book, you might think the number-one worry of retirees is outliving their money. While that is certainly a major concern, surprisingly, it appears that the single biggest fear is deteriorating health. This is perfectly rational. Good health offers a freedom few people appreciate until they no longer have it. Health is one of those things we tend to take for granted until life takes an abrupt turn for the unexpected and health suddenly becomes an issue.

To ignore one's health in the single-minded pursuit of money or, worse, to abuse one's body in the pursuit of wealth is frankly a foolish proposition. If you break through the financial independence finish line with oodles of cash and an enormous investment portfolio, it will be a Pyrrhic victory if that financial wealth comes at the expense of your physical or mental well-being, or indeed your relationships.

Perhaps it's more than just a coincidence that the terms health and wealth are practically homonyms (they sound the same, save for a different letter at the beginning of each word). We'd go so far as to say that health *is* wealth, but not the reverse; we don't believe that wealth is health. Just ask any multi-millionaire who's on death's door. All the cash in the world can't buy back health that has been lost. You can't put a price on health. You may not perceive your present vibrant health as an asset, but you'll surely realize it as that if you suddenly lose it. Remember our earlier discussion on human capital: human capital presumes a healthy body and mind that allow you to convert that capital into financial capital.

The good news is that Victory Lap is a holistic concept that spans the whole spectrum of the post-corporate lifestyle. It's as much about health as it is about wealth, which means that when planning your Victory Lap you must ensure that it includes exercise, proper diet, relationships, and—as chapter 10 will explore—the spiritual dimension.

As this book neared completion, Mike's mother was residing in a nursing home. Spending time visiting her there, Mike was able to observe first-hand the many benefits of having good health by observing so many people who have so little of it. It really hit home for him that without good health it doesn't matter how large your investment portfolio is. We spend so much time and energy saving and worrying about whether we will have enough money for retirement; but the reality is that if physically you can't get out of bed, does it really matter what you can afford to spend your money on? The truth is that if you cannot meet the physical demands of the adventures you've dreamt about and saved for, you are just as poor as the person who didn't save and can't afford to go on those adventures.

It was these kinds of considerations that prompted Jonathan's subtitle for his book *Findependence Day* and the tagline for the Financial Independence Hub: achieving financial independence "while you're still young enough to enjoy it." Sure, a common response to financial insecurity is to "just keep working," but can you really count on perfect health well into your sixties or your seventies?

Those visits to the nursing home served as a wake-up call when Mike realized it's only a matter of time before we all succumb to stroke, heart attack, cancer, Parkinson's, Alzheimer's or other forms of dementia, or some other age-related illness. But he also knows we can increase the odds of enjoying more quality years if we keep our bodies fit, our minds challenged, and our hearts engaged. Your Victory Lap is a special time in your life that affords you the time, money, flexibility, and vitality to do all of those things. This is a time to take care of you all-around, and to live life to the fullest on all fronts. As a result you may just find that the Victory Lap years are the richest, happiest, and most rewarding time of your life.

PLAN TO BE HEALTHY

Each of us has the power to improve our health so we can continue to do the things we love today for many years to come. In the end it's all about personal choices we make regarding activity, involvement, and attitude.

Generally speaking, over the years baby boomers have learned to take better care of their minds and bodies than the generations that preceded them. They tend to eat more sensibly and most are well aware of the value of regular exercise. Indeed, the trend to healthier eating is apparent in the North American restaurant business. While fast food chains stagnate, there is a whole new wave of companies that cater to healthy eating and healthy living. Meanwhile, makers of colored, sweetened water— Coca-Cola and Pepsi—are scrambling to move their product lines to more healthy choices in beverages or snacks.

The boomer generation has a narrow window left in which to travel and enjoy other pursuits before their possibilities are curtailed by health issues. On average, people will make it only to age sixty-seven without some form of disability that will moderately or severely limit them. Data from Statistics Canada show there is a one-in-three chance of someone in the 65–74 age bracket being disabled, which means not being able to work or move about freely. In fact, people are more likely to become disabled than to die prematurely. The bottom line is that disease is unpredictable and you need to enjoy life while you still can.

Medical issues that prevent people from working are wide-ranging and often caused by being stressed out and overextended by work and other responsibilities. This can lead to debilitating conditions like depression and anxiety. On the physical side, those who are overweight are more likely to develop type 2 diabetes and be vulnerable to related complications like heart disease or stroke. Well-being guru Dr. Lesley Horton blames our increasingly sedentary lifestyles and poor diets for the fact that roughly one-quarter of the population is considered obese. This is the idle generation: many already sport pot bellies, "muffin tops," and double chins. Those who exhibit these visual signals have a heightened risk for cancers and other serious diseases. There is even a new term—diabesity—which refers to being afflicted with both diabetes and obesity.

Upon leaving the Corp, some may choose to buy a comfy recliner, upgrade the cable package, or binge-watch the latest hot shows on Netflix. But by spending most of your time sitting around munching on snack foods, sooner or later your health will pay a steep price. Why act older than you really are? Smart people realize that to have a high quality of life they must challenge themselves every day. You can't just settle in and kill time, waiting for the end. You need to take an interest in yourself and extract every ounce of life's possibilities. Make the decision to thrive, not just survive!

LIFE EXPECTANCY AND LONGEVITY

A big theme in this book is that of extended longevity, not just for the baby boomers but also for their children—the millennials and/or Generation X. We believe the combination of an exercise regime, healthy eating, and continued breakthroughs in medical science and biotechnology means people are going to live a lot longer than we once might have imagined. Therefore, our primary careers may last a good long time, and

it also means we have time to plan properly for a well-rounded Victory Lap, one that could last anywhere from one to three or more decades.

Traditionally, financial planners have pencilled in ninety as a target age for making an investment portfolio last. Obviously, some people will die before that age and others will die after it. Spend some time reading the obituary pages of any newspaper and you will witness the trend toward rising life expectancies. While disease, accident, and sheer bad luck may take us off the stage in our forties or fifties, or even before that, there are plenty of centenarians breaking past age 100 and even a fair number who make it to 105. While the oldest recorded human in modern history is France's Jeanne Calment (who reached 122), it's not hard to imagine some of the millennial cohort living beyond that age, perhaps to 125 or, as some predict, even age 150.

We suggest that when conducting your financial planning you ask your financial adviser to work out a "what if?" scenario for you by adding ten years to your expected lifespan. If, for example, you always figured you'd live to age eighty-five, readjust your thinking and imagine living to ninety-five instead. How will that affect your planning, your retirement date, and your financial projections?

EXTEND YOUR WORKSPAN *AND* YOUR FUNSPAN

It's one thing if your "bonus" years afforded by breakthroughs in longevity are spent in declining health, but entirely another if you also gain extra vibrant, healthy years. If healthy living and eating, and avoiding harmful habits like excess consumption of drugs, alcohol, or tobacco, do grant you some extra years of life, it's likely that most of those years will be healthy and potentially productive ones.

If your what-if exercise of tacking on ten more years to your life expectancy opens your eyes to the possibilities, we would suggest splitting the difference: allocate five of those extra years to work (your "workspan") and another five to leisure, or what we call your "funspan." After all, is it not logical that if you are going to have an extended *lifespan*, you also have an extended *workspan*? The fact is that you will more than likely need to continue working longer than you may have planned just to finance that longer life you'll live. So, for example, if you once believed you would "retire" at sixty-two and live to eighty-five, try to imagine you and your spouse living to ninety-five. Take half the extra ten years and assign them to your workspan, meaning that you now plan to work in some fashion or another until age sixty-seven instead of age sixty-two.

This does not have to be more years in the corporate cubicle, though of course if you're in a congenial workplace you might actually want to stay there. There are huge financial advantages to staying in the company pension plan an extra five years as you also let your investment portfolio grow for another half decade and delay the receipt of government benefits like Social Security or the Canada Pension Plan.

But if you had your heart set on stepping off the corporate hamster wheel by age sixty-two, you can still do that without embracing a full-stop retirement. This may be the time to implement your own version of a Victory Lap: start your own business; create a website; reinvent yourself to become a novelist, painter, stand-up comic, or public speaker; go back to school to study theology; enroll in medical school; become a lawyer—whatever your long-suppressed dream may be. Or maybe you'll do something you had never contemplated in your youth but now realize may be perfect for you in your Victory Lap incarnation.

NEVER STOP LEARNING

At some point, extended physical health may mean the long-term threat is no longer to your body but to your mind. The older you get and the longer you live, the greater the odds are that you or your partner may be attacked by the twenty-first century scourge of dementia, and in particular Alzheimer's disease, which is having an increasing presence in the lives of North Americans, including in our popular culture. One such example is the novel and film *Still Alice*, which vividly portrays the plight of a university linguistics professor who suffers from early-onset Alzheimer's. While the cause may be genetic in only a small number of cases, this is another area where scientific research is pushing the boundaries.

In the meantime, just as we have learned to take care of our bodies by eating well and exercising, we should take the trouble to keep the brain limber and active. The brain is a muscle that needs to get a daily mental workout. This is one reason we believe in encore careers even for those who leave the corporate world. The workplace provides both mental and social stimulation that has to be a positive for the brain. Just having a sense of purpose every morning when you awake is a good reason for continuing to stay active in the workplace, if only on a part-time basis.

But even if you embrace a "full-stop" retirement by your mid-sixties, eschewing paid work of any kind, you still should never stop learning. Take night-school courses at a nearby college or university. Learn a new musical instrument. One of our friends took up the clarinet after taking early retirement in her mid-fifties, for example. We know a former financial adviser of the same age who was counseled by a life coach and finally revived a childhood dream of becoming an actor. Today, he has an agent, has appeared on the silver screen in a film short, is active making TV commercials, and is well on the way to creating his own theatrical productions.

Entire books describe how to keep the brain active and keep dementia at bay for as long as possible. Perhaps you had a childhood passion for a game like chess that you can rediscover. You can play chess with anyone in the world at any time by playing online, and bridge players can do the same. Others will like to play Sudoku in the daily newspaper. It doesn't really matter which of these activities you choose; the point is to emulate the fictional detective Hercule Poirot and keep "those little gray cells" active.

THE POWER OF A POSITIVE ATTITUDE

An extraterrestrial visitor to twenty-first century North America would no doubt be baffled by what it observed of the privileged citizens of the United States and Canada. Despite all our wealth, labor-saving devices, and technological marvels, very few of us are truly happy. We distract ourselves with alcohol, drugs, television, gambling, shopping, and so much more. More people die by their own hand than are murdered. We are much better off today than at any other time in history, but surveys confirm that most employees are unhappy at their jobs, with depression rates getting higher year over year. Something is seriously out of whack.

The apparent explanation is that we live in an increasingly stressful and negative world and most of us just don't know how to deal with it. People naturally tend to focus on the negative, and of course the news media tend to emphasize whatever is going badly in the world. As journalists quip about news judgment, "If it bleeds, it leads." Terrorism and the 24/7 news cycle tend to leave even the most optimistic among us somewhat anxious about the future. Add in economic and financial insecurity, and it's little wonder that even affluent North Americans worry about the future.

Those of you still accumulating wealth may wonder why seemingly "rich" folk often keep working. We can tell you that those with large portfolios of cash and bonds worry about interest rates, while those with large portfolios of stocks or equity funds worry about another crash in the stock market, and both groups worry about the potential for high inflation! If anything, those with lots of money tend to worry about it more than those who do not have as much. Over time, what goes into our minds, the experiences we have had, and what we flood our minds with becomes our reality. We become what we think about all day long. Therefore, having a pessimistic attitude will make you susceptible to depression, higher stress levels, and poor health. Odds are that unless you take proactive measures to counteract this negative mindset, it will result in a shorter lifespan.

You can adopt a positive attitude about life or you can choose to remain on the dark side. You can make a conscious decision to focus on the positive and filter and control what goes into your mind. You can reduce your mind's exposure to violent television shows or movies and negative people who constantly moan and complain, and instead train your mind how to focus on the positive and the hopeful possibilities in every situation. Try to surround yourself with successful, positive people who will serve as a good role model and encourage you to chase your dreams. Look forward to each new day just like you did when you were younger, with an attitude of joy and wonder. Life is wonderful if you look at it the right way.

A happy corollary of this is that optimists tend to do better in business, whether they are working for someone else or running their own business. So if you plan to be an entrepreneur during your Victory Lap, you'd be well advised to think like an optimist, if you don't already! If you're an investor, focusing on the positive is more likely to permit you to enjoy good investment returns. As any financial adviser will tell you, in the long run you will make higher returns with stocks than bonds and cash, but to buy and hold stocks, you need to have a certain amount of faith and confidence in the future. Generally, that faith will pay off if you're disciplined enough to invest for the long run.

Instead of fretting about all the bad things that can happen, focus on what you want in your life and be grateful for all the things that you already have. Optimism *can* be learned, as positive psychology guru Martin Seligman reminds us in his book *Learned Optimism: How to Change Your Mind and Your Life*. Or read Shawn Achor's book *The Happiness Advantage: The Seven Principles of Positive Psychology that Fuel Success and Performance at Work*, which presents a useful paradigm shift: happiness is not something that can be deferred until after you succeed in life; be happy here and now and that positive attitude will contribute to your eventual success.

Remember that, as in the dictionary, happiness comes *before* success! Too many of us place happiness at the back of the bus. Why do we tend to defer happiness and push it further out? We delude ourselves that we will be happy once we pay off the mortgage, or after we save another $500,000 for retirement. Why can't we just be happy now?

The answer is that you can find ways to be happy now (read or reread the story of the Mexican fisherman at the end of the next chapter for an illustration of this idea). The truth is that being happy means you are more positive. When you are positive you are sharper, have more energy, and are more motivated to accomplish your goals. Try to remove your focus on money and accumulating a certain level of capital by a certain date; instead, relax and start living again—just like the Mexican fisherman. Don't compete with others or be tempted to keep up with the proverbial Joneses. Focus instead on practicing gratitude, it will help your attitude immensely.

When you're running a Victory Lap, instead of being competitive (as in the corporate world) you need to think in terms of self-improvement. Competitiveness means competing with *others*, while self-improvement is about competing with *yourself*. It's very hard to get competitiveness out of our blood, as many have been in that environment all their working lives. Who hasn't had to endure sales contests and quotas or grade fellow workers on a bell curve that permits only a tiny minority to "exceed expectations" on performance reviews? Business leaders seem to have created an environment in which we always have to beat the other guy or gal. It's like we're all Roman gladiators doing battle in the Colosseum.

Most of us were taught to chase the money, and even in the Victory Lap it can prove hard to get away from that mindset. Instead of thinking about money all the time (as a payback for your time), think about how good you will feel when you help someone, and have fun whether or not you can cut an invoice at the end of the activity.

In short:

- Have a good attitude, be a positive person, and try to make at least one person smile every day.
- Have a sense of humor and laugh every day.
- Develop an attitude of "If they can do it, I can do it."

Go back to having a beginner's mindset about life, similar to how a child views the world. Be curious and keep growing because of that curiosity.

Aging Is a Matter of Attitude

Your attitude determines how you approach life and how you experience it. You can only accomplish what you *think* you can achieve. You likely can recall the children's story about the "little train that could," or how some people believe they can do an Ironman triathlon because the approach they take to goal-setting is, "Anything is possible if you want it badly enough." What we do and what we are depends on what we think.

Today you are where your attitude has *brought* you, while your future is where your attitude will *take* you. Even aging is largely a matter of attitude. You can be seventy-five and still act like you are forty-five; or you may be only forty-five chronologically yet be perceived as acting like you're seventy-five. Refuse to be defined by age. Optimists live longer than pessimists, and this alone can add up to an extra seven-and-a-half years, on average.

Successful aging is about having a positive attitude toward aging. It's about having something exciting to look forward to and knowing what it takes to keep going mentally and physically, challenging yourself every day. No pain, no gain. This is partly what doing a Victory Lap is all about. Staying engaged and active, possibly even continuing to work, will give you purpose, fulfillment, a sense of accomplishment, and just enough of the challenge you need to keep yourself vibrant. Make it fun. Laugh at yourself: You're like a kid again! Hang around positive people who are attempting the same things you are. Stay away from boring, negative people. With them, it's like trying to save a drowning person—they just might take you down with them!

Dwelling on your problems rather than your possibilities is not the way to go through life. See the half-empty glass for what it is: half-filled. Be a positive person and you'll be healthier and happier than the pessimists. It makes no sense worrying about past events or mistakes unless you want to experience them for a second time (or more).

Control Your Mind and Stay in the Moment

The secret of health for both mind and body is not to mourn for the past, worry about the future, or anticipate troubles, but to live in the present moment wisely and earnestly.
—Buddha

Most of us are so focused on the future that we don't realize the beauty of the moment. We tend to drift through our days, guided largely by habits and routines, not really listening to or noticing what is happening around us. We hear things but don't focus on what they really mean. When we are home our thoughts are focused on work issues; at the office our minds are focused on what is happening at home. We need to slow down and focus on the present moment, to enjoy what we are doing while we're doing it.

What you focus on will determine your destiny, so it's important to use self-discipline and focus on the good stuff. Stop taking life so seriously. Take the time to watch a beautiful sunset; hear the silence around you. Appreciate what is all around you and appreciate each moment to its fullest. This problem of always being in a hurry to get somewhere usually gets worse as we get older.

DON'T PURSUE HAPPINESS, DISCOVER IT

Our souls are not hungry for fame, comfort, wealth, or power . . . Our souls are hungry for meaning, for the sense that we have figured out how to live so that our lives matter, so that the world will be at least a little bit different for our having passed through it.
—Rabbi Harold Kushner

Victory Lap Retirement allows us to change from a "surviving mentality" to a "thriving mentality." A happy Victory Lap Retirement is not a commodity that can be bought in a store or online: it needs to be well thought out and planned so that it is the perfect lifestyle for you, unique to your needs, goals, and situation.

For his part, the American motivational speaker Zig Ziglar made a practice of trying to brighten the moods of strangers through random acts of kindness each day. When you make someone else smile you end up smiling too. The very act of giving to others makes you feel better as well. Give it a try and see for yourself.

Happiness occurs when you understand that what you are seeking isn't to be found outside of yourself. You can't buy it, borrow it, or even steal it. Happiness is already inside you, waiting to be rediscovered. No matter how much you have in the bank, how many toys you have, or how much you earn, none of it will make you happier in and of itself.

If you know what must happen in order for you to be happy, why don't you just do it? Most of us will be unable to answer this question, as it's easy to get sidetracked: life gets in the way, bills need to be paid, and we tend to let our dreams slip away and lose hope for the future. When you eventually wake up and begin to live your life intentionally (literally "on purpose"), you will discover there is no better feeling than when you do something that you love; something that excites you and makes you realize that your contribution matters.

All of us have been given clues as to our purpose during our lifetime. We need to go back, review the tapes, and figure out our unique strengths, skills, and talents. Remember what it is that gets you excited and what you are passionate about, then figure out how it all fits together and what you want to be so you can live up to your full potential.

If you didn't discover this during your primary career, you definitely want to take advantage of your Victory Lap to do so. Once you discover your true calling you will know exactly where you want to go and what you plan on doing when you get there. The key is to stay in alignment with your purpose, passion, and your mission. Once you figure out and align "who you are" with "what you were born to do," you can't lose!

Having purpose is great for the soul. It makes you feel good and gives you a reason to get out of bed in the morning (remember the power of *ikigai*?). You need to create a sense of purpose for your life after full-time employment. It's about challenge and fulfillment, finding the perfect combination of striving and accomplishment that comes from achieving a big goal. Without purpose, life is meaningless.

After leaving your primary career and entering the Victory Lap, you need to feel that you still matter, that you're not invisible to the world but are still contributing to society in some form. People become passionate when they can tap into things that really matter to them. A happy life requires a fair degree of passion. Without it, life is without meaning.

Remember, true wealth is health. Having a Victory Lap Retirement will enrich your life, but you need a healthy body to run the race. The fact that a well-executed Victory Lap will also provide you with additional income and a larger nest egg is a bonus, but remember that the real payoff is the purpose you will find for yourself and live by every day.

10

Spiritual Health

One thing you can't hide is when you're crippled inside.
—John Lennon

Closely related to physical and mental health are emotional and spiritual health. Even if your parents have blessed you with a flawless genetic heritage and a robust physical body, these will count for little if you abuse those gifts with destructive habits and practices.

To us, physical health flows from mental health, and mental health in turn flows from spiritual health. All the money in the world will be of little comfort if your spiritual life or mental outlook isn't healthy. Recent news stories about the affliction of "affluenza" affecting the offspring of rich parents should be a cautionary warning about this: abundant financial wealth is no substitute for a solid moral compass that all parents should pass on to their children.

There are many different spiritual practices that you can adopt to nourish your soul and contribute to your overall mental and physical health. Like your Victory Lap in general, your spiritual practices should be customized to suit your own personal needs and preferences. The point is that in this stage of your life you are probably better positioned to focus on this aspect of your well-being than at any other time before.

FIRST, PUT YOUR FINANCIAL INDEPENDENCE INTO PRACTICE

The first practice we recommend focusing on is consciously acting like the independent person that you are. But it's not as easy as you think. It may take some time before you can fully accept your hard-won independent status and start acting like the financially free being you have worked so hard to become. You must psychologically and emotionally embrace your financial independence before you can translate it into actual behavior that fully takes advantage of the freedom you have so long pursued. Making some space in your life to focus on your spiritual health can help you get into that independent frame of mind.

As we saw a little earlier in the book, a big part of the Victory Lap idea is your own attitude. Author Robert Gignac put it well in the title of his financial novel, *Rich is a State of Mind: Building Wealth and Happiness—A Blueprint.* We can similarly assert that "financial independence is a state of mind." It doesn't matter how big your retirement nest egg is if you don't think you have enough to step off the corporate treadmill.

We know first-hand how hard it is to break the working habit upon crossing the finish line of financial independence. The law of inertia means that bodies already in motion tend to stay in motion, so the initial response to sudden financial freedom is often to keep pursuing dollars. In Jonathan's case, his first entire year after reaching financial independence was dedicated to the "just keep working" philosophy. Technically this wasn't absolutely necessary, as he was in the fortunate position of having no mortgage, no consumer debt, and enough money in the bank to take an extended sabbatical. And to top it all off, he was (and is) blessed by a wife who continued to work full-time. Mike's situation was similar.

In many ways, this impetus to keep working is perfectly understandable. Achieving true financial independence may take between twenty-five and forty years of practicing the good old work ethic, keeping one's nose to the grindstone of employment, and maintaining the frugal behavior that makes independence possible. It takes a hard-working, hard-saving attitude to lay the foundation of financial freedom, and living your life according to this attitude can be a hard habit to break. In Jonathan's case, it wasn't until the end of June 2015—by which time this book's first writing had begun in earnest—that he really started to experience the more relaxed mindset of "work because you *want* to not because you *have* to," truly embracing the part-time freelance lifestyle that he preached in *Findependence Day*. You can also call this the "Work Optional" stage.

Looking back, it's not hard to see why this happened. Jonathan had spent a quarter of a century drawing a regular salary from just two employers, both of whom became clients after he reached financial independence. No wonder it took him a year to actually enjoy a stretch of free time as well—the first time in ages that he had neither an employment contract nor a short-term contract to provide writing or editorial services.

Running a Victory Lap is freedom, certainly, but it may not be quite the exhilarating feeling of liberation you may imagine you'd experience on receiving a gold watch on your sixty-fifth birthday at a traditional retirement party. How quickly you embrace your financial independence—and start living the lifestyle it allows—will vary with temperament, age, and family circumstances. If your spouse and friends are all still working, it may seem natural to continue to do so yourself. But recognize that, to a large extent, remaining on the money treadmill may by this point be largely a self-imposed activity. Work has a momentum of its own: after all, for many years it was an absolute necessity.

One discovers in the Victory Lap that work continues to be an important component of this new lifestyle. But instead of it being the master, now it is you who is master and work becomes your servant. Relishing the time, space, and flexibility you have worked so hard to achieve in your Victory Lap can take many forms, and you'll need to figure out which practices are best for you. But we're willing to bet that making room for some or all of these in your life will be good for your soul.

BUILD IN ELECTRONIC DOWNTIME

Taking care of your spiritual health can be as simple as "getting off the grid" from time to time. Here in the twenty-first century, we are blessed by technological gadgets and "devices" that can serve as marvelous productivity aids. Indeed, the millennial generation has been raised on the internet, smartphones, and sharing services, and they seem lost without their devices. But there's a place and time for using these machines. Our consumer culture offers no end of distractions, from television to movies to social media, all of which compete for tiny slivers of our attention and thus our life energy.

In theory, it costs nothing, either in money or effort, to still the mind and filter out all external stimuli. But society offers so many distractions and demands on our attention that looking within is anything but easy for the average citizen of western industrial democracies.

One easy way to conserve your life energy, or win some of it back, is to build a little electronic downtime into your Victory

Lap. Try to walk outside without a Fitbit, smartphone, or any other electronic devices. Instead of connecting with people you've never met through social media, see if you can boost your life energy by using some more of your time to connect with your inner self.

Establish at least one room in your home as an electronics-free zone, free from the lights and sounds of most of the other rooms. It's difficult these days, but ideally your bedroom should have a minimum of lights and screens, including TVs, computers, tablets, or cell phones. Exposure to digital device screens affects the quality and duration of your sleep because of how the light emitted from the screens interferes with the body's ability to produce melatonin. And so, the more screens are eliminated from the period leading up to your bedtime, the better your sleep will be.

Even ten minutes every morning of attempted meditation (more on this practice below) should yield some fruit in terms of peace of mind and equanimity. If a dedicated meditation room is not for you, perhaps a particular designated space could do double duty for reading, yoga, or other forms of exercise. These introspective pursuits are a subtle thing and may not be for everyone at a particular stage of life. But remember that once you're off the treadmill and have experienced a modicum of independence on your Victory Lap, you may be ready to entertain activities you rationalized you "never had the time for" while you were still spinning the corporate hamster wheel.

A good substitute for those who find it difficult to look within is instead looking outside yourself by appreciating nature. Jonathan, for example, lives within fifty yards of Lake Ontario and not a day goes by without a walk or bike ride along the lake (or in the winter, ice skating near the lake). It's been said that the most positive brainwave activity can be generated by a nature walk and the simple act of appreciating natural beauty. Let the blue tranquil calm of the lake or the quiet green cathedral of the forest reflect your mind at rest.

MINDFULNESS

In trying to get yourself into the Victory Lap mindset, you might consider incorporating mindfulness and mindfulness meditation. Whether you are working full-time or not, mindfulness is a powerful tool for nurturing a positive attitude, honing your focus, and creating overall well-being. While meditation is generally practiced for ten or twenty minutes once or twice a day, mindfulness is something that can and should be practiced throughout the day (see also chapter 8, Time as a Resource).

One book we'd recommend is Maria Gonzalez and Graham Byron's book on equanimity and mindfulness, entitled *The Mindful Investor: How a Calm Mind Can Bring You Inner Peace and Financial Security.* (We could, of course, turn that descriptive subtitle on its head by observing that if you already possess financial security, then it can bring you a calm mind and inner peace.)

Either way, mindfulness is all about maintaining a positive attitude and focusing on the present moment, not just during your more formal morning or evening meditation practice (more to come on that shortly). Whatever activity you are engaged in at any given time, try to "be" with that activity, including "work" tasks and money-making activities. Stay focused on the task at hand, trying not to let the mind be dragged into dwelling on the regrets of yesterday or the anxieties of tomorrow.

In the 1960s, the counterculture guru Ram Dass (formerly Harvard University's "acid" researcher, Richard Alpert) epitomized the requisite attitude with his famous classic book, *Be Here Now.* Whether you're still working full-time or have started to enjoy the more leisurely pace of the Victory Lap, you should always strive to make time to still the mind and reflect.

It may be easier to devote time to these activities during the classic full-stop retirement, when there are fewer excuses for failing to take the time to look deep inside one's soul. By its very nature, business (i.e., busyness) is a distraction that prevents us from discovering our true selves. Once work is no longer such a commanding part of our lives, there's no longer an excuse not to discover our true selves. This is a good thing, so embrace the opportunity.

Certainly, though, compared to the frantic years of one's primary career, the more balanced years of Victory Lap Retirement are more conducive to the kinds of spiritual practices we describe. While it would be lovely to spend forty-five minutes every morning and another forty-five minutes every evening in deep meditation, few of us will have that kind of time (or commitment), even in the Victory Lap. Just ten minutes every morning is better than no minutes at all, and if you're still working full-time, even five minutes can be beneficial. Start small, be open to trying it (there are various smartphone apps that can help with your breathing and related disciplines), and if you start to get results, you can increase the rate and frequency of your sessions. Or you can attempt to move on to dedicated time for meditation.

Try to train your consciousness to be aware of the present moment; to be free of regret about the past and free from worry about the future. So, for example, if you're eating some tasty food, focus on the taste and don't start thinking of what you'll do once you've finished eating. If you're talking to a friend, be with that person and really listen to what he or she is saying. If you're looking at a sunset over a lake, be with the sunset. Spiritual writer and meditation advocate Paul Brunton advocated experiencing both sunrises and sunsets, bookending every day with a spiritual, aesthetic appreciation of nature that far transcends the hubbub of commerce and the daily bad news.

START YOUR DAY RIGHT WITH MEDITATION

Earlier we introduced the idea that there's really only one day. It's helpful to start that day—every day—with some spiritual discipline. It's important to make time to escape the noise of the world, and when better to do that than immediately upon rising at the start of that day? There is something magical about the first few hours of the morning. Time seems to slow down and a deep sense of stillness and calm fills the air.

Each of us needs to make a daily commitment to spend time in a quiet place so we can restore clarity to our world and become centered again. During this time we need to reflect on who we really are, and remember what's important and what's not. We talked about the importance of living in the moment and of cultivating a positive attitude. Meditation helps us to achieve this state of mind, slowing us down and clearing our mind of distractions, allowing us to remember all the good things in our lives. In meditation we can hear our inner voice and reconnect with who we really are. Use meditation to empty the mind of all worries and negative thoughts. Instead, focus on the positive aspects of your life, what makes you truly happy. It's there, but often you are just too busy to be aware of it.

You can easily add meditation to your morning or evening routine (or prayer and meditation, if you accept the notion that prayer is speaking to the almighty and that meditation is listening to the response). A morning or evening (or both) spent in meditation or contemplation can set you up for the whole day, helping you visualize and plan for it. Then at the end of the day you can look back and reflect on the experiences and lessons learned, the personalities you encountered, and the challenges that can be renewed the following day.

Over time you will begin to see things differently, new ideas and opportunities will appear, and you will find ways to make your dreams come true. Without dreams and something to look forward to, it's hard to find a reason to get out of bed every morning. Start to listen intentionally to your inner voice and intuitions, learn to trust them, and become aware of all the possibilities around you. Trust your inner self and listen to what it is trying to say to you, then create a path aligned with your goals and dreams. This is your personal Victory Lap customized to the unique individual that is you! Small daily steps over time will get you there.

Most of us have been in survival mode for too long. In Victory Lap you have a chance to once again gain control over your life. Now is the time to be intentional with your life. It is no longer okay to go through it just surviving, it's time to really live and enjoy everything life can offer.

JOIN A COMMUNITY OF SPIRITUAL SEEKERS

If you feel you lack the discipline to get started on these kinds of practices on your own, seek out groups that can act as your spiritual support group. Finding or rediscovering a community of fellow spiritual seekers may provide a double benefit—not just in facilitating your growing spiritual side, but also in connecting with a community of like-minded souls. This could be in the form of the traditional church, mosque, or synagogue whose attendees meet on Sundays (or in some cases, Saturdays), or it could be less formal organizations, like yoga or pilates groups, for example.

The latter are springing up just about everywhere. Take advantage of the low-cost introductory courses many offer to beginners; you can become acquainted with the different practices and instructors and find those closest to your temperament and lifestyle. At the same time, you will start to meet some of your neighbors who have a similar approach to life. Some yoga centers even have designated "soul coaches," so there's a lot more to these mind/body practices than just contorting the body into various poses!

If you're more community-minded, you may choose the path of helping others through volunteering or philanthropy, donating your time and energy to hospitals, food banks, service clubs, senior communities, hospices, or any number of worthy organizations. In so doing, you may well discover the truth that in getting outside of "self" and devoting your energies to others, your own problems appear smaller.

Those who are more intellectually inclined may choose simply to read about philosophy and religion, although again one might find more stimulation by taking an extension course at a nearby university. The advantage of meeting others with similar interests will be a bonus.

Part of keeping the mind active and never ceasing to learn is reading, although this is largely a solitary activity. The local library is one of the great bargains out there: you can order the books you want online and they will be held for you, to be picked up on your next visit. Or you can download free e-books or audio books through services like OverDrive.

We know a group of middle-aged women who have a rotating book club, with the members taking turns once a month to host a light dinner and sample the wine cellar. It's as much a social event as it is a literary one, but like many other activities mentioned in this chapter, it serves a dual function: keeping the brain active for solitary reading while also bringing together a community of like-minded individuals.

BOREDOM VERSUS STRESS

Earlier we talked about boredom being the elephant in the room in retirement. Much of the Victory Lap Retirement lifestyle is about taking advantage of the time flexibility conferred by financial independence. During the wealth accumulation years, stress is often our constant companion. Just holding down a full-time job, raising a family, and keeping the home fires burning is enough to keep the average North American fully occupied for decades.

For many, boredom is something many couples *wish* they could experience. This is perhaps why the traditional advertising message of full retirement seems to appeal to many of us: we've been so stressed out working and raising families that the idea of doing nothing at all at the end seems quite alluring—until you actually get there. We know quite a few early retirees, some fortunate enough to have been pensioned off by their early or mid-fifties. After a few months of "doing nothing," most start looking for part-time work, going back to school, preparing for a new encore career, or contemplating creating a business. (Recall Rob's experience with early retirees at his colleague's golf club.)

The danger is that you can soon find yourself overcommitted even in a well-executed Victory Lap. There's a fine line between boredom and stress. For the most part, the full-time primary career and associated family life is mostly filled with stress, which is why we advocate stress-reduction practices like exercise, proper diet, and spiritual disciplines like yoga or meditation. By contrast, the classic full-stop, do-nothing retirement may be at the opposite extreme: not enough stress, and hence boredom, whether it comes soon or later.

The beauty of Victory Lap Retirement is that you can design it right from the get-go with the proper mix of work and leisure. And to do that, you may well need a team to coach you. We all know about financial advisers, accountants, tax lawyers, and the other professionals who can help you achieve financial independence. But equally, we may need the services of "softer" advisers: life coaches, soul coaches, personal trainers, and even consultants who are specialists in decluttering or organizing files and emails.

For us at least, Victory Laps are about taking our private dreams to a new, higher level. For Jonathan, the original point of financial independence was to allow time to do creative projects like novels (*Findependence Day* being the first of these) or the non-fiction book you are now reading. *Victory Lap Retirement* does meet our criterion of a long-term creative project that hopefully will add to the world's literary stores in a way that will resonate with at least some readers.

THE POWER OF GRATITUDE

If the only prayer you said in your whole life is "thank you,"
that would suffice.
—Meister Eckhart

Prior to starting his Victory Lap, Mike wasn't thrilled about how he was living his life. He felt like he was just killing time, waiting for eventual retirement while feeling stuck in a job he no longer loved. Every day it was the same routine. He and the Contessa would get up early, go to work, get home, make dinner, watch TV, then repeat the same cycle over and over. Days turned into weeks, weeks into months, months into years, and before they knew it they felt like they were among the walking dead.

Luckily, Mike has a pretty smart wife who could sense his unhappiness and she pushed him to do something about it before it destroyed him. Even though he would have to give up a good-paying job and resigning early would mean a reduced pension, she reminded him there were more important things in life than just having the ability to buy more stuff. Somewhere along the line Mike had forgotten this. But when he finally decided to set out on his Victory Lap, his attitude began to change and he started to see the world differently.

Over the years we become so focused on what we *think* we need to acquire to achieve happiness that we forget to be grateful for what we already have, what we've already accomplished, and what's really important. When we think about gratitude we're reminded of the old Persian proverb, "I wept because I had no shoes until I saw a man who had no feet." It's so easy to magnify our problems and lose sight of the many blessings for which we all have to be thankful. We must stop taking things for granted and realize what a great life we already have. Having gratitude is so powerful: it has the ability to transform your thinking from negative to positive, which in turn will enhance your well-being.

To increase your own sense of gratitude, it can be very helpful to create a list of all the things for which you're grateful. Your list will be unique to you and should contain all the important things in your life for which you're deeply grateful and that will assist you to face whatever you have to deal with today.

Mike's gratitude list looks like this:

• I'm grateful I was born in Canada, one of the greatest (nicest) countries in the world.
• I'm grateful to have married Melina, one of the most caring, loving people in the world. She continues to amaze

me each and every day and I love having the opportunity
to build a life and business together with her.

- I'm grateful for our three wonderful children and can't
  wait to see what great accomplishments they will achieve
  in the years ahead.
- I'm grateful I have found a second career that has given
  my life purpose and a high degree of personal satisfaction.
- I'm grateful that Rob and Jonathan decided to partner
  with me in writing this book, which I know will help so
  many people.
- I'm grateful to be in a position to help others achieve
  happiness in finding their true passions, and to help take
  the fear out of retirement planning.

In addition to having a gratitude list, it's a good idea to start a
gratitude journal. This will serve to train your brain to focus
on the many positives in your life, the things that really count.
Each day try to list at least three positive things that happened
to you that day. It may be hard at first and there may be a great
deal of repetition early on, but it will force your brain to review
the tape from the last twenty-four hours and search out positive,
meaningful events or people that you encountered, things you
otherwise might have forgotten or taken for granted.

Over time you will start to see and appreciate the small things
that add up to a happy life and realize how blessed you really are.
Things like the taste of a good meal, going on a slow walk after
dinner with your spouse, and taking the time to enjoy a sunset
will take on an increased significance. Life is pretty good when
you take the time to think about it. So whenever you start to feel
anxiety, envy, or worry creeping in, you'll be able to pull out your
gratitude list and remember what is really important in the grand
scheme of things. Gratitude will win out every time.

Mike searched the world over for happiness and contentment, and finally discovered it was in his backyard the whole time.

HOW MUCH IS ENOUGH? THE TALE OF THE MEXICAN FISHERMAN

Asked to define "wealthy," most financial advisers would probably define it in terms of money and their clients' ability to buy things that supposedly will make them happy. However, becoming wealthy is much more than having obtained a certain amount of money. True wealth is based on personal satisfaction and having the freedom to live life on your own terms. It's the kind of freedom and satisfaction you gain from running a Victory Lap once you are financially independent.

An instructive example of true wealth can be found in the story of the Mexican fisherman, originally told by the German writer Heinrich Boll in 1963. Since then, it has been re-told and adapted by many. It's a classic tale about the general theme of living in the present, and the folly of forever "slaving and saving" today for the mirage of a single one-time-and-forever "retirement" in the far-off future. (All on the assumption that employers, pension managers, financial markets, health, spouses, and family will cooperate.) This apocryphal tale often finds its way into financial books, and it's a parable that never fails to amuse us, even after multiple readings. To us, it epitomizes the difference between working to live, and living to work.

The protagonist of this little fable is a humble fisherman. The antagonist is a rich American investment banker who visits the fisherman's pier located in a small coastal village of Mexico. A little boat with just one fisherman is docked by the pier. Inside the boat are several large yellowfin tuna. The American compliments the Mexican on the quality of his fish and asks how long it took to catch them.

"Only a little while," replies the Mexican.

The banker is curious as to why he didn't stay out longer to catch still more fish, and the fisherman replies that he has enough to support the immediate needs of his family.

The American then asks, "But what do you do with the rest of your time?"

The fisherman replies, "I sleep late, fish a little, play with my children, take siestas with my wife, Maria, stroll into the village each evening where I sip wine, and play guitar with my amigos. I have a full and busy life."

To this, the banker—who among other things possesses a Harvard MBA—scoffs incredulously. He tells the fisherman he should spend more time fishing and buy a bigger boat. "With the proceeds from the bigger boat, you could buy several boats; eventually you would have a fleet of fishing boats. Instead of selling your catch to a middleman you would sell directly to the processor, eventually opening your own cannery. You would control the product, processing, and distribution."

Of course, there's one small catch: to do all of this the fisherman would have to leave his small coastal fishing village, move to Mexico City and ultimately New York in order to run the thriving enterprise.

Dismayed, the fisherman asks how long all this would take. He's told fifteen or twenty years.

"But then what?" the fisherman persists.

The American laughs and says, "That's the best part. When the time is right you would announce an IPO and sell your company stock to the public and become very rich, you would make millions!"

"Millions—then what?"

"Why, then you would retire," the banker replies triumphantly, pointing out that the fisherman could then move to a small coastal fishing village in Mexico, sleep late every day, fish whenever he wished, play with his kids, take siestas with Maria, stroll to the village to sip wine in the evenings and play guitar with his amigos.

It's a killer punchline—though in real life the kids would have to be replaced with grandkids, the amigos would be long gone, and the odds are 50/50 that by then the beleaguered fisherman would be paying alimony to Maria. Even so, this story really resonates with us, and with almost anyone we know who has encountered it. This is because it clearly demonstrates what wealth is and isn't. It reminds us that true wealth has more to do with *feeling* wealthy rather than having accumulated a certain level of assets.

What constitutes feeling wealthy? How about having good health, having a congenial spouse, having a loving relationship with your family, having a few really close friends, having the freedom to spend time doing what you want to do when you want to do it? A wealthy man is content with what he has. If you want more than you have, you are not wealthy.

Throughout our lives, we have been taught that success is based on a person's net worth and the accumulation of things. We have been conditioned by the advertising industry to believe that buying a new car or the latest gadget will make us happy. But this happiness is fleeting and there is always a new advertisement about a better car, better gadgets, and all the other trinkets of modern society. We need to step back, clear our minds, and determine what is really important to us. We need to realize we may already have enough and become content with the life we are living now instead of the lifestyle being sold to us by advertisers.

What does having "enough" mean? It starts with having achieved sufficient financial freedom that we feel secure enough to choose meaningful work regardless of compensation. For Mike, enough means he can finally stop chasing happiness and contentment, as he already has it; he just didn't see it. He now knows he is richer than those who have more money but lack the understanding to enjoy what they have worked for.

Enough means having enough to live, enough to be happy, enough to chase your dreams. Now you can stop spending so much time making a living and focus solely on making a life, because you finally realize that you have enough.

11

The Final Chapter

How Would You Like Yours to Read?

Twenty years from now, you will be more disappointed by the things you didn't do, than by the things you did do. So throw off the bowlines. Sail away from the safe harbor. Catch the trade winds in your sails. Explore. Dream. Discover.
—Mark Twain

NO REGRETS: LIVE AN UNCOMMON LIFE

One of the saddest things that can happen to people is suddenly realizing in the twilight of their lives that they feel a great deal of regret over a life only half lived. Recently we read a book written by palliative care nurse Bronnie Ware. Over the years Ware had recorded the regrets of her dying patients, and she shared the information in her book *The Top Five Regrets of the Dying: A Life Transformed by the Dearly Departed*. According to the book, the number one disappointment shared by Ware's patients was, "I

wish I'd had the courage to live a life true to myself, not the life others expected of me." Many people follow the path that their parents or teachers thought would be best for them and, in so doing, they gave up their own personal dreams. They realize too late that they should have taken the more risky or the more fulfilling job, for example, but for whatever reason didn't.

This theme runs through a recently published book called *Sixty: The Beginning of the End, or the End of the Beginning?* by Ian Brown. After noting his sixtieth birthday with a long post on Facebook, Brown kept a journal for his entire sixty-first year and the result seemed to encapsulate the dilemma of his generation: we all seem to be running out of time to achieve what we thought we were going to do when we graduated from college more than half a lifetime ago. It's even more poignant when you look at the relatively early deaths of some major creative artists who *did* live the life of their dreams, like Eagles co-founder Glenn Frey or the iconic David Bowie, who passed away at sixty-seven and sixty-nine respectively.

This theme also seems to tie into a Gallup poll that found 70 percent of people hate their current job, according to the survey results published in a 2011 *Forbes* article. Clearly, something is not quite right here. For many people, dreams go unfulfilled because of earlier choices they made or avoided making. If you wish to prevent this kind of regret in your life, you need to start making the right choices so you can leave this world with peace of mind.

For example, changing from a job you don't like to one you love, even if it means earning less money, makes sense because the quality of your remaining life will improve. (Jonathan once took a $25,000 cut in pay in order to leave the lucrative field of public relations and re-enter the field of journalism, which he found much more satisfying. Over the years, he made up the short-term hit and then some, but the real benefit of finding a more congenial occupation cannot be measured in dollars and cents.)

The second most common regret in Ware's book was, "I wish I hadn't worked so hard." People deeply regretted spending so much of their lives at work, where the focus was primarily on making money. They wished they had spent more time with their family and friends, and they regretted taking life so seriously all the time. Along the same lines, a regret of Mike's—or maybe we should call it guilt—was when he looked back and realized he had spent the best years of his children's lives climbing the imaginary ladder of success at the Corp in pursuit of security for his family.

Always remember the greatest gift you can give to your family is the gift of your time, of you! Many of us tend to forget this; we are so busy just trying to survive that we end up investing most of our time in our jobs. Unfortunately, Mike can't go back and change things, but he, for one, plans on spending the rest of his life making up for lost time. The guilt will always be there, but he intends to bury it under many new experiences he plans to share with his family and the amazing memories they'll continue to make together.

The third most common regret was, "I wish I'd had the courage to express my feelings." Many people go through life with their opinions and emotions bottled up inside. They feel they can't say how they really feel because it might make them look weak. It's important to tell your kids and your spouse on a regular basis that you love them. There's nothing weak in doing that. Saying you love someone is one of the most impactful things you can say to another person, and it doesn't cost a cent.

The fourth most common regret was, "I wish I had stayed in touch with my friends." Long-term friends are priceless. Building these deep relationships takes time and it's a downright sin to let these connections slip away through neglect or feeling that you are too busy to maintain them. Make long-term relationships a priority in your life because they will pay off large whenever you need them.

The fifth most common regret was, "I wish I had let myself be happier." It's unfortunate that many people wake up and realize only late in life that happiness was always up to them to create. Real happiness depends on adopting a lifelong positive attitude. And, as we saw in the two previous chapters, your happiness also depends not on pursuing some external ideal but on finding it within yourself. You are responsible for your own happiness, and the sooner you realize this, the sooner you'll be truly happy.

Statements like "I wish I had made more money" or "I wish I owned more things" didn't make it into the top five lifetime regrets. Puts things in perspective, doesn't it?

After reviewing the tapes of your life, you will probably find the most regret will flow from the risks that you did *not* take, the opportunities that you did *not* pursue, and the fears that you let control you because you didn't have the courage to face them. It's important to realize that fear inhibits us and prevents us from living a wonderful life. While we still have the time, we need to break free of our self-imposed fears; we have to get out of our comfort zone, stop playing it safe and take more risks. Stop being so focused on chasing and maintaining security, and instead focus on chasing opportunity. That's when a person really starts living. The saddest words you will ever hear are, "I could have been . . . if only I had . . . ."

For whatever reason, most people fail to live out their dreams. They remain in survivor mode waiting for something to happen that will change their lives for the better, but nothing ever seems to materialize. As the years go by, they become frustrated and bitter. If you want evidence of this just visit any retirement home and sit at the table occupied by the complainers. You can't miss it—it's the table with all the sour faces.

In her book *Silver Boxes: The Gift of Encouragement*, Florence Littauer described her father's lifelong desire to become a singer and the sad fact that he never became one. She said he died with the music within him. Not attempting to become the person you know you should be is like dying with the music still inside you.

It's a shame to simply endure and complain about life or to miss out on it altogether; instead, take risks and squeeze every bit out of life that you can. Our time on earth is way too short, or maybe it's better to think of it as too fast. We all know how it ends, so why not do some cool stuff while you still have the chance? And that's what your Victory Lap is for—living life to the maximum now that you're financially secure and while you're still young enough to enjoy it. Remember, each of us has the power to choose the kind of life we want to live. Choose to be happy or choose to live with regret; the choice is yours alone.

THE GREAT CIRCLE OF LIFE

Mike's father taught him a lot of basic lessons early in life: study hard, work hard, save your money, avoid debt, and take care of your family. He was the teacher and Mike the willing student. But now Mike finds that it is his mother who is filling in the remaining blanks, imparting some of the lessons his father never had the chance to teach him. His mother's recent journey from retirement home to the nursing home has been an eye opener: Mike is finally starting to understand that happiness and a sense of fulfillment come from within.

Things seem relatively meaningless when we come face to face with our ultimate destiny, which is apparent at every visit Mike makes to that nursing home. Looking back, there was a progression: each move his mother made—from detached house, to retirement home, to nursing home—resulted in a shrinking of her living space and a corresponding reduction in her possessions. Now she has only a few pieces of furniture left, pictures of her family that adorn the walls, and memories. You begin to realize that somewhere along the way things got messed up. Surely we were not born just to die, leaving a big pile of unused, discarded consumer junk behind. Why did we buy all that stuff in the first place?

When life is boiled down to its essentials, it becomes easy to separate what's important from what's not; you realize money is not the most important thing, nor are the items it allowed you to purchase over the course of your life. What's really important, what really matters, are the memories we created with our friends and families, and the lives we have touched and tried to help—all the people who hold a special place in our hearts.

Mike watches his mother sometimes when she sits staring

blankly at a wall. He wonders what she's thinking about and on what meaningful moments in her life she is focused. One day he and the rest of us will be in her shoes, assuming we live that long. We'll review the tapes, judging whether we made a difference in other people's lives, living on our own memories. Whether we will be remembered, and how we will be remembered, is what really matters.

The thought of possibly living with some level of regret over lost dreams or missed opportunities is scary, so Mike made a promise to himself to invest the rest of his time on this planet chasing his own dreams, helping people in some fashion, and making wonderful memories with his wife, kids and, hopefully one day, grandchildren. Mike is running the awesome Victory Lap that he designed intentionally for himself.

IT'S YOUR STORY: WHY NOT WRITE A HAPPY ENDING?

Our job in this life is not to shape ourselves into some ideal we imagine we ought to be, but to find out who we already are and become it.
—*Steven Pressfield*

The tragedy of life is not death but what we let die inside of us while we live.
—*Norman Cousins*

Every year around Christmas, Mike looks forward to watching the movie adaptation of *A Christmas Carol*. It's based on the Charles Dickens classic about the mean and miserable Ebenezer Scrooge, a money lender who constantly bullies his poor clerk, Bob Cratchit, and rejects his nephew Fred's wishes for a merry

Christmas. Scrooge lives only for money, has no real friends or family, and cares only about his own well-being. As the story goes, on Christmas Eve Scrooge is visited by three ghosts that teach him the lessons of the Christmas spirit through his visions of Christmases past, present, and future; in each visit he sees either the negative consequences his miserly nature has created or the good tidings that others bring about through their love and kindness. Scrooge sees his future death: dying alone, with no one to mourn him. He has his money and his possessions, but nothing else. He finally understands why qualities like generosity and love are some of the most important things in life. He is grateful when he realizes he has a chance to redeem himself and change his future. This is the important message conveyed by the film: if Scrooge can change and improve his future life, then anyone can change theirs.

Imagine the satisfaction you could have if you arrived at the end of your days knowing that you did everything you possibly could have done in order to live the life you wanted. Put some thought into how your Victory Lap can help you do this, both for yourself and the people closest to you. Don't be like most people who finally figure out how to live while lying on their deathbed, suffering from regret.

The timing of *A Christmas Carol* is perfect for Mike as it puts him in the right frame of mind for the annual review he and the Contessa conduct at the end of December. It's a reminder of what's really important and what's not: that it's all about what a person accomplishes in life. Not in terms of making money or acquiring things, but how a person has helped and touched the souls of others. It's a reminder that we still have a last chance to be remembered as we want and that we need to start living that way today. All of us have control over how we are going to live from this day forward and the quality of your life will depend upon the choices you make each and every day. (And remember there's really only one day to do all these things, and that day is *today*.)

So somewhat like Scrooge, you can give yourself the power of choice, but in this case by designing and executing the Victory Lap you want to live. It's not too late to choose optimism, action, and the pursuit of a life well lived. Do you like the way you are currently living? If your current job adds a lot of stress to your life, adopting a Victory Lap philosophy might be the answer you have been looking for—an escape route to a life and work that you find deeply fulfilling.

It's important to understand that the only risk bigger than starting a Victory Lap is staying in a stressful job that you dislike. How much stress does the job add to your life? How does it impact your relationship with your family and friends and your quality of life? Why become a work zombie doing a job you hate for money that you really don't need, half of which, for those in the top tax brackets, is taxed away? The government will thank you for your generous support of the treasury department, and your heirs may welcome a hefty inheritance, but what about the squandered life energy and relationships that could have instead been cultivated in a balanced Victory Lap?

In working with clients to prepare their financial plan, Rob and his colleagues often find that financial independence is an elusive concept, so much so that many are prone to put it off and continue accumulating as much as they can, "just in case." Although this is a prudent and practical thing to do, the reality is that they're only working hard and stressing out to increase the pile of money that will be left over after they've gone. I often stop clients in their tracks by saying, "You can keep working, but the likelihood is that all you're doing is increasing the size of the estate you'll leave behind." This can be a watershed realization.

If, by careful calculation, you have enough assets and income to make a break for it, why would you wait to retire if continuing to work won't ultimately change anything about how you live over the next twenty, thirty, or forty years?

Mind you, if you're fortunate enough to have a high-level corporate career for which you have real zest and passion, that's quite another matter. Your Victory Lap might allow you to continue to go down that same path but gradually reduce the number of days or hours you work. Perhaps you'd take your expertise to other Corps that could benefit from you being a board member or a consultant. The networking opportunities that result would be part of a well-planned Victory Lap for these kinds of high achievers.

Think about all the wealthy people in the world who do not have to work, but who still choose to do so: Warren Buffett and Bill Gates come to mind, both of whom have committed their late-life careers and the bulk of their wealth to philanthropy. The reason they continue to work is because they love what they are doing. Like them, we have no intention of retiring and our adventure is not over. This is something we should all strive for and Victory Lap will help get you there.

Why worry about your health or about running out of money when you can do something about it? People generally don't take charge of their own life because the easiest way to deal with change and all the anxieties that go with it is not to deal with it at all. We act this way to avoid responsibility and because we're not willing to make an effort. You need to be different and to take action.

So don't waste time fretting about things that don't matter. Instead, focus on the things that really matter—family, enjoyable work, health, and fun experiences. Your plan should be to squeeze out every last remaining ounce of life that you can. Don't squander your last chance to chase your dreams in Victory Lap. Get out of your comfort zone and really start living again. Stop playing it safe and start dreaming big, like when you were a kid. You're not too old to try something new, all you need is the courage to start. Believe us, you won't regret it!

We wrote this book for people who are not satisfied, and who want more. For the people who are saying to themselves, "Hey, I'm not done yet." By choosing to do a Victory Lap, you are willing to make changes to a story that is still only partially written. Why not write a happy ending for yourself? You can if you choose to! It's all up to you.

"DASH" DINNERS

Along the lines of writing your own final chapter is the idea of having a "Dash Dinner," a celebration of life that focuses not on the dates of your life and death on your tombstone to tell your story, but on the dash in between that refers to what you did and accomplished in life.

So here's the idea: as you approach your Victory Lap, retirement, or any other significant life change, consider hosting a "Dash Dinner" event with your best friends and family to celebrate. These events done in conjunction with a retirement are a great opportunity to have attendees raise a glass and toast the honoree by sharing a story or trait they admire about that person. You can imagine how the guest of honor (perhaps you) would feel hearing such stories and gratitude from the people closest to them!

WHERE DO WE GO FROM HERE?

He who has a "why" to live can bear almost any "how."
— Friedrich Nietzsche

After reading this book, you can no doubt now see that we have all been seduced into believing that the traditional full-stop retirement is the answer for a wonderful life. After all, they tell us, isn't that the reason we worked so hard over the years, so one day we would be able to sit back and do nothing?

We've been culturally brainwashed to accept retirement as the answer to all our problems. We all bought into the deal: work hard for thirty-five years and then you can finally begin to enjoy a wonderful life in retirement. After reading this book you probably realize that retirement is a relatively new phenomenon. It's the carrot, an invented need, an artificial solution to a man-made problem that's in direct conflict with our natural instincts.

We have all been sold on the need to work hard and save like crazy over a long period of time, then to hit the brakes and do something inherently unnatural: retire. No wonder we are so stressed out. Work is an essential part of life: people need to be able to contribute, they need to interact and socialize, and they need to have a good reason for getting out of bed in the morning. Full-stop retirement is not the best answer for many.

If you think like us, it's okay to say you like to work; it's okay to stop doing what *they say* will make you happy, and do what *you know* will make you happy. Find work that makes life interesting and fun. Create a lifestyle based on some combination of work and play that gives you what you need. As we say on the cover, you want the flexibility to play while you work and to work while you play. If you've really designed your Victory Lap properly, you'll barely know the difference between work and play. Congenial work *is* play! Life doesn't have to be so difficult and unsatisfying, if you choose to be intentional and take steps to create a great life. Having the chance to pursue your true purpose, how can you argue with that? How can you lose?

Most of us haven't even scratched the surface of what we want to be, what we wish to achieve, and what we want to contribute—and that's what gets us up each and every morning. Who knows what new ideas and possibilities will come to us during our respective Victory Laps? The beauty of being in Victory Lap is that now we control our own days and set our own agenda. We don't do anything we don't want to do, and that puts a big smile on our faces!

So there you have it, a new approach to maximizing the quality of your remaining years. You have paid your dues, you have met your responsibilities to your family, and now it is your time to create that lifestyle you always dreamed about. You can make it happen if you want to; you are more than capable, and the decision is yours and yours alone. So what are you waiting for?

Acknowledgments

The authors wish to thank the following people for their contributions, knowledge, and other help in creating this book.

MIKE

First and foremost I would like to thank my beautiful wife, Melina, whom I affectionately call "The Contessa," for standing beside me while I went a little crazy writing this book. She is my rock, the love of my life, and I dedicate this book, or at least my portion of it, to her.

To my father, Stanley Drak, who taught me my first Victory Lap lessons, and to my mother, Viola Drak, who continues to show me the way.

To my kids, Doug, Danny, and Austin, for encouraging me and for helping me solve all of the many computer problems I encountered while writing this book.

To Ernie Zelinski, whose book *How to Retire Happy, Wild, and Free* motivated me to start on this journey. Ernie has been, and continues to be, a great mentor to both Jonathan and me. We are lucky to have him in our corner, as can be seen in the Foreword he graciously penned for this book.

To Tom Deans for taking the time to show us the ropes and for encouraging us to take the book on the seminar circuit.

Special thanks to Robert Ott for helping us come up with a great name for our book!

And lastly, to my co-authors. Rob, it's been a pleasure working with you on this second edition. Your professional expertise in retirement planning has added great value and more financial discipline to the book, and it's been fun having you along for the ride. Jonathan, you convinced me to write the book in the first place and it was a lot tougher than I thought. But the hard work is behind us and the fun starts!

ROB

Thanks to my wife and best friend, Emily, for not just supporting my efforts but being my constant thought partner on all subjects, especially this one. You first came up with the term Victory Lap while we were driving!

To my partners at Huber Financial, especially Dave Huber, who have backed me at all times and in every way. Also to Martha, you've been the ultimate executive producer, bringing this book to life.

To my Dad, who not only taught me how to connect with people and make a difference for others, but was also the first person I saw to live a Victory Lap. Your success inspired me to work with others to make it work for them too!

To my many clients and friends, whose lives and stories have helped me see this as the future of retirement. Thank you for letting me learn from you and partner with you.

And lastly, to Mike Drak. You reached out to me and have been a great partner to work with on this book. Thank you for the opportunity!

JONATHAN

To my wife, Ruth, and daughter, Helen, who keep hoping every book will be my last. They're my reason for getting up in the morning.

Thanks to our editor, Karen Milner, whom I finally got to work with after a few earlier almost-deals in our previous publishing incarnations.

To Steve Nease, for creating the compelling cartoons that will provide some comic relief during the reader's jog through the pages of *Victory Lap Retirement*.

A special thanks to "Eagle Eyes" Christopher Cottier, the best technical editor around when it comes to financial books. And to David Chilton, whose generosity to fellow authors continues to astound.

And last but certainly not least, to my co-author, Mike, whose enthusiasm for this project overcame my initial doubts about attempting yet another book.

JOIN THE *VICTORY LAP RETIREMENT* TRIBE

The way we practice retirement is changing rapidly and we are heading into unmapped territory, where the retirement status quo and old stereotyping no longer apply.

If after reading this book you are like us, and thinking about retirement in new and exciting ways, consider joining our tribe at:

www.victorylapretirement.com

You'll find a community of like-minded adventurers, as well as weekly blog articles focusing on retirement lifestyle planning and the psychological and emotional side of retirement transition.

Our tribe members are retirement rebels, the pioneers of huge retirement change—people who live way outside their comfort zones, showing us what is possible. We care for one another and challenge each other to find clarity and meaning in retirement.

Retirement is too big and important a life change to go it alone—join our tribe to be inspired, and create and share your own vibrant and fulfilling Victory Lap!

WE CAN HELP YOU LEAVE THE RAT RACE BEHIND AND RUN YOUR OWN VICTORY LAP!

Mike Drak is living the dream, running his own Victory Lap and making it his mission to help others do the same. He is available for speaking engagements, seminars, workshops, and also provides one-on-one retirement coaching. For more information, please contact Mike at:

michael.drak@yahoo.ca

Rob Morrison, CFP,® is President of Huber Financial Advisors, LLC, an independent wealth management firm headquartered in Lincolnshire, Illinois. If you would like Rob to speak about Victory Lap Retirement at an industry conference or present a seminar to your group, please contact him at:

rmorrison@huberfinancial.com

More information about Rob Morrison and Huber Financial can be found at www.HuberFinancial.com or through the company's social media pages on LinkedIn, Twitter, and Facebook.

ABOUT THE AUTHORS

Michael Drak is a thirty-eight-year veteran of the financial services industry and lives with his wife, Melina (also affectionately known as "The Contessa"), in Toronto. He started his own Victory Lap in 2014 and is busy helping others transition into their own personal versions. In addition to mentoring others, he gives speeches and seminars to groups across the country and cultivates and maintains the Victory Lap community at www.victorylapretirement.com.

Rob Morrison, CFP,® is a CERTIFIED FINANCIAL PLANNER™ professional and President of Huber Financial Advisors, LLC, in Lincolnshire, Illinois. He has been a wealth manager for nearly twenty years and has coached many clients through their Victory Lap transitions. Rob is a passionate advocate for his clients navigating the changing retirement landscape. His article titled, "Preparing for a Victory Lap," was published on Morningstar.com and he appeared with Christine Benz, Morningstar's director of personal finance, in a video about the same topic. Rob is actively engaged in the Victory Lap community at www.victorylapretirement.com.

Jonathan Chevreau is a veteran financial columnist, blogger, and author. He was personal finance columnist for the *Financial Post* (1993-2012), and editor-in-chief of *MoneySense* Magazine (2012-2014). Since declaring his Findependence Day (the day he became financially independent) in 2014, he has been blogging for the Motley Fool, Financial Post, and MoneySense.ca, and launched the Financial Independence Hub in 2014, a website that covers the topic from a North American perspective. He has published U.S. and Canadian editions of his financial novel *Findependence Day*, and is also the author of *The Wealthy Boomer* and several editions of *Smart Funds*.